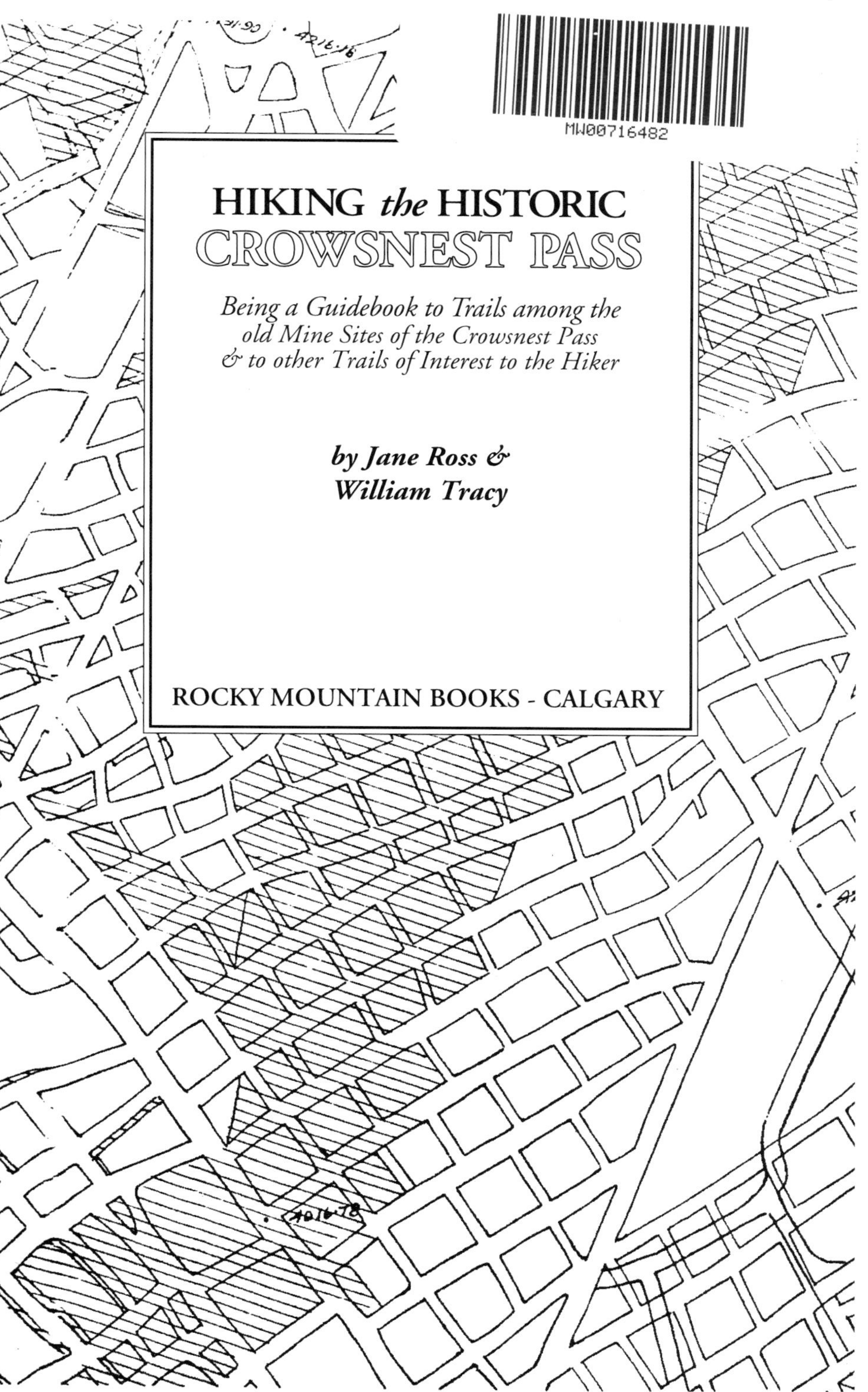



# HIKING *the* HISTORIC CROWSNEST PASS

*Being a Guidebook to Trails among the old Mine Sites of the Crowsnest Pass & to other Trails of Interest to the Hiker*

***by Jane Ross & William Tracy***

ROCKY MOUNTAIN BOOKS - CALGARY

*Front Cover: Crowsnest Mountain from McGillivray Ridge.*
*Photo Gillean Daffern.*
*Back Cover: Bernard Coke Ovens at Lille.*
*Photo William Tracy.*
*Title Page: Mine plan courtesy of the Provincial Archives of Alberta.*


Second edition, 2001



We acknowledge the financial support of the Government of Canada through the Book Publishing Industry Development Program (BPIDP) for our publishing activities.

Printed and bound in Canada by
Houghton Boston, Saskatoon.

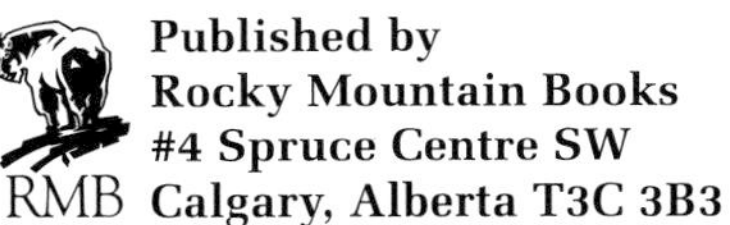


**National Library of Canada Cataloguing in Publication Data**

Ross, Jane, 1948-
Hiking the historic Crowsnest Pass

Includes bibliographical references and index.
ISBN 0-921102-78-X

1. Crowsnest Pass (Alta. and B.C.)--Guidebooks. 2. Trails--Crowsnest Pass (Alta. and B.C.)--Guidebooks. 3. Hiking--Crowsnest Pass (Alta. and B.C.)--Guidebooks. I. Tracy, William, 1950- II. Title.
GV199.44.C22A458 2001 917.123'4043 C2001-910012-4

# *Contents*

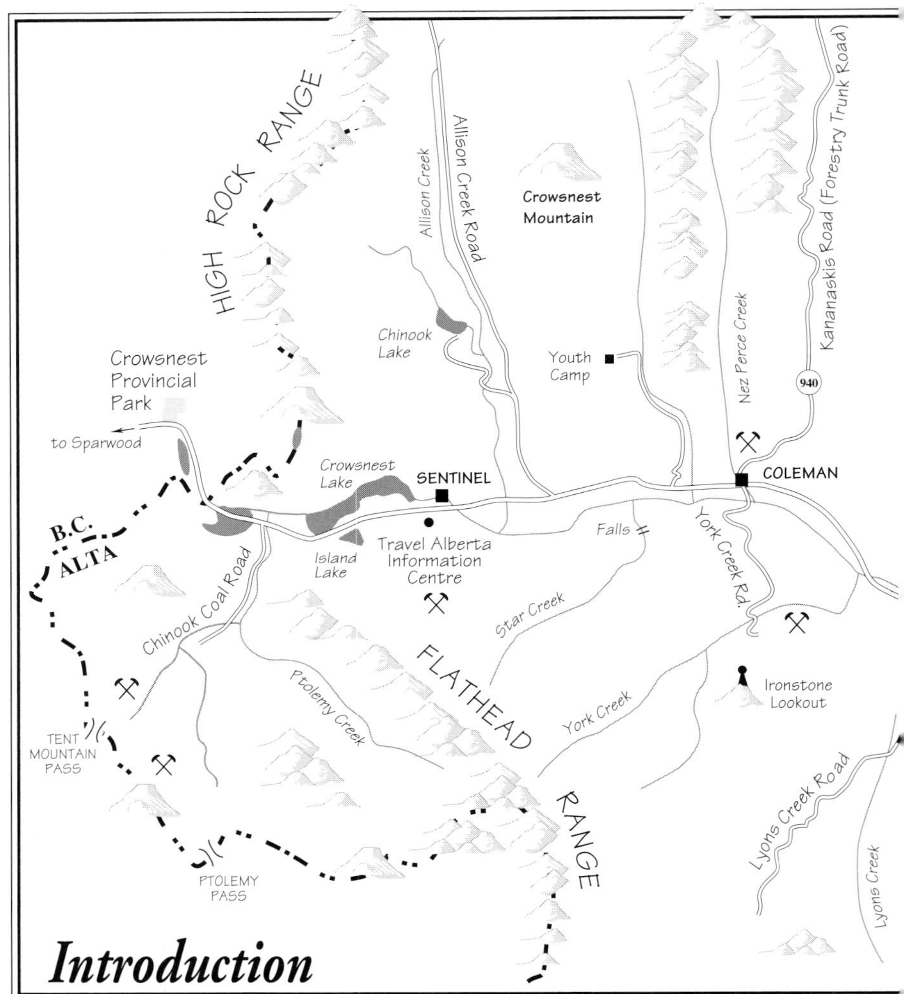


# *Introduction*

In central and southern Alberta, the unique geology, flora and fauna of the Rocky Mountains are protected from development through the establishment of national and provincial parks and reserves. One after another, they stretch down the spine of the Continental Divide: Willmore Wilderness, Jasper National Park, White Goat Wilderness, Banff National Park, Siffleur Wilderness, Ghost River Wilderness, Peter Lougheed Provincial Park, Kananaskis Country, Rocky Mountain Forest Reserve and Waterton Lakes National Park. There is only one small break in this sequence. Lying between Waterton Lakes National Park in the south and Kananaskis Country in the north is the Crowsnest Pass.

The Crowsnest Pass was first mentioned in the written record by Captain Blakiston of the Palliser Expedition in his 1858 preliminary report where he reported a nesting

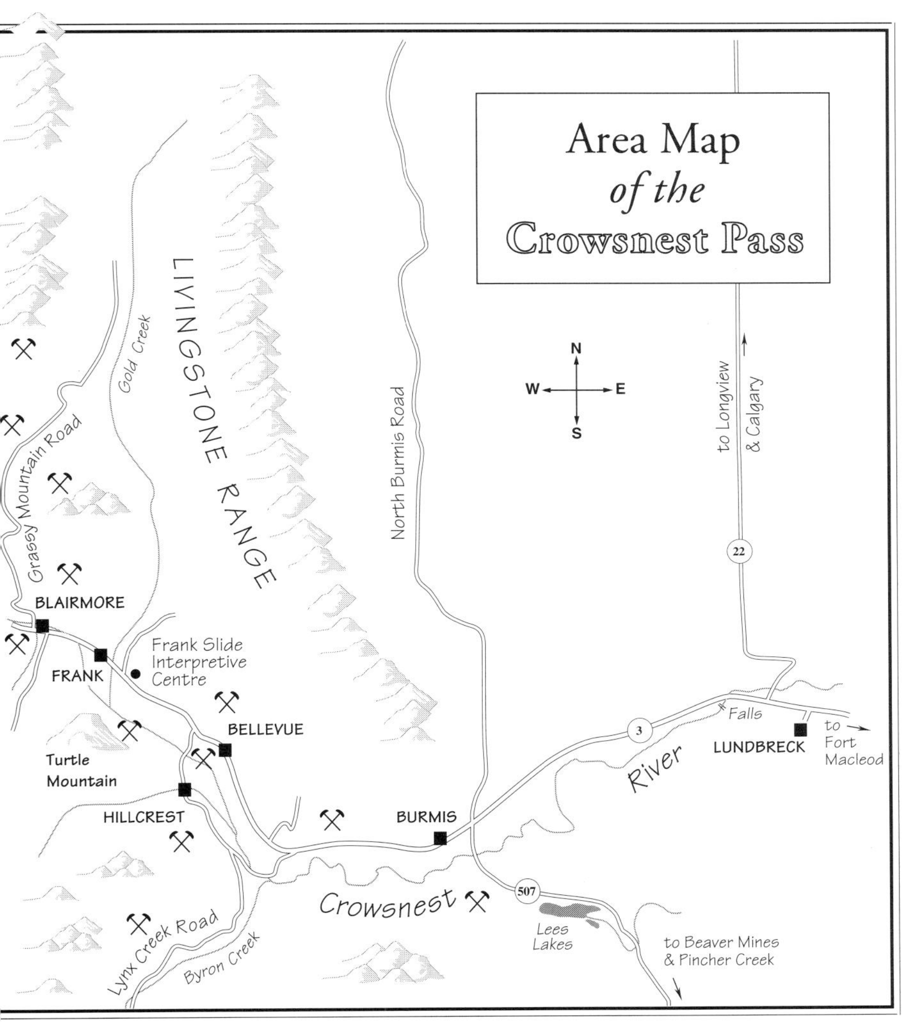


site of ravens—lodge des corbeaux—at the base of a certain mountain. It is probably from this source that the name "Crowsnest" is derived, although there is an unsubstantiated story that a band of Crow Indians, trapped by pursuing Blackfoot, was massacred at the base of the mountain that now bears their name in memory. Whichever explanation may be correct, the name Crowsnest has been given to the entire pass, as well as to a prominent mountain, river, creek, lake and other geological features.

The most southerly of all the major transportation passes that cross the Rockies, the Crowsnest stretches from Lundbreck on the Alberta side to Sparwood in British Columbia. Its landscape is dominated by two geological zones, the foothills and the Front Ranges. Approaching the pass on Highway 3 from the east, the limestone wall of the Livingstone Range signals your arrival. Beyond here, the mountains are low with rounded profiles, heavily wooded on north and east slopes yet have numerous open, inviting ridges and slopes facing south and west. At the west end of the pass, on both sides of the Great Divide, the high peaks of the High Rock and Flathead ranges compare favourably with those found in the national parks, though none are glaciated.

The Crowsnest Pass escaped park or reserve designation owing to the early exploitation of its coal seams. Located in great bands that lie perpendicular to the pass, the coal seams increase in thickness and number as you move west and south. The Canadian Pacific Railway was particularly interested in the pass' potential as a source of good steam coal, for it needed the fuel to fire its engines across the prairies and over the mountains. Others became interested, too, especially after the Canadian Pacific Railway laid its branch line through the pass in 1897-98, thereby opening the area to possible development.

The years between 1900 and the outbreak of war in 1914 were heady ones. Immigration was at an all-time high. Homesteads were being snatched up by immigrants from Europe and the United States. New towns with their support businesses were springing up almost overnight. The future appeared to be boundless.

It was in such an atmosphere that entrepreneurs, willing to undertake the necessary financial risks, moved into the Crowsnest Pass to develop the coal seams. The first company to exploit the rich seams was the Canadian-American Coal and Coke Company, which opened the Frank mine in Turtle Mountain in 1901. Once the quality of coal had been proven, the rush to develop the reserves was on. In 1902, Charles P. Hill obtained control of the mineral and surface rights for a mine at Hillcrest, followed the next year by three companies: West Canadian Collieries, which opened its first of five mines at Lille; Breckenridge and Lund who opened a mine farther to the east; and the Galbraith Coal Company of Lundbreck, which developed the seams at the easternmost end of the pass. These companies were followed within a few years by the large and successful International Coal and Coke Company, which established itself in 1903 south of Coleman; the Leitch Collieries, which opened a seam on Byron Creek in 1907; and McGillivray Creek Coal and Coke Company in 1909, which opened the seams north of Coleman. A number of small companies also attempted to exploit the wealth of the area. Many were paper companies only, never extracting so much as one tonne of coal; others folded after a year or two.

The halcyon days ended abruptly with the onset of World War I. Coal companies that relied on the sale of coke to Europe suddenly found themselves without an attainable market. It did not take long before a number of them, already over-extended owing to their capital development and fierce competition, were forced to close. Only the West Canadian Collieries' mines, those of International Coal and Coke, McGillivray Creek Coal and Coke, Hillcrest and a few others that operated sporadically over the next decade remained in business after 1915. After the war, sales continued to shrink as the railway companies began their switch to diesel fuel, forcing most of the remaining companies out of business. Those that survived did so because of amalgamations. The last operating mine on the Alberta side of the pass, located in Coleman, closed in 1983.

Today, the mountains that once throbbed with industry are quiet. But physical reminders of that long-ago era can still be found throughout the mountains and valleys of the Crowsnest, enabling the hiker to appreciate the impact coal mining had on the environment and on the people who depended upon it. It is this rare combination of historical ruins and fine scenery that makes the Crowsnest Pass a unique place to hike.

The delights of hiking in the pass are well known to those people who live there, but not to outsiders. Because it lies beyond any park boundary and was once heavily industrialized, the Crowsnest Pass has not become a tourist mecca like Banff and Jasper. While it is not unusual in the pass to share a hiking trail with others, you can often enjoy a ridge walk or a tramp in the woods by yourself. Routes are reasonably well delineated but unmarked, a number of them following social trails or trails along open ridges. Others follow old mining and logging roads that are now impassable, even for four-wheel-drive vehicles. Because logging is still an important industry in the pass, access to some hikes may change slightly. Always remain alert to logging trucks when driving logging roads still in use.

The variety of scenery is astounding and ranges from the forests and grassy ridges of the Eastern Portal and Livingstone Range to the scree slopes and high alpine meadows of the Flathead and High Rock ranges. As you might expect, there is a wide variety of wildlife inhabiting these different zones. Mule deer, elk and moose are commonly seen. The flora, too, is unusually interesting as the pass acts as a transition zone between Waterton Lakes National Park to the south and Kananaskis Country and Banff National Park to the north. Some species of flora and fauna found in the extreme southern part of the Front Ranges are not found north of the pass, and likewise, species found farther north are not always found south of the pass.

Depending on the previous winter's snowpack, the hiking season generally extends from mid-April to mid-October. So when is the best time to hike in the Crowsnest Pass? It all depends on what you want to experience. If poking around historic ruins appeals, then early spring is an excellent time before leaves and vegetation hide many of the artifacts. If wildflowers or wildlife fascinate, then come in late spring and summer. And if it is the high alpine country that draws you, late summer or autumn is often more suitable, remembering that the pass is outside of the national parks and autumn brings the hunters.

The Crowsnest area is renowned for the strong winds that funnel through the pass at all times of the year and can reach speeds in excess of 100 kph. Wind is perhaps the most important factor you will want to bear in mind in planning a ridge walk or an ascent of Crowsnest or Turtle mountains. The wind, too, can signify a change in the weather for the worse, so always carry rain gear. In the pass the weather is often localized. If it is raining in the Flatheads, chances are the trails at the eastern end of the pass are dry. But should bad weather interfere with your plans, there are a number of excellent tourist attractions, eateries and pubs, all listed at the back of this book.

Finally, please respect both the natural environment and the historic sites so that others can enjoy, learn and inherit.

Jane Ross and William Tracy

## DISCLAIMER

There are inherent risks in hiking in wilderness and semi-wilderness areas. Although the authors have alerted readers to locations where particular caution is to be exercised, trail conditions may change owing to weather and other factors. Abandoned mines and other buildings or sites may be unsafe. Hikers use this book entirely at their own risk and the authors disclaim any liability for any injuries or other damage that may be sustained by anyone using any of the trails or visiting any of the sites described in this book.

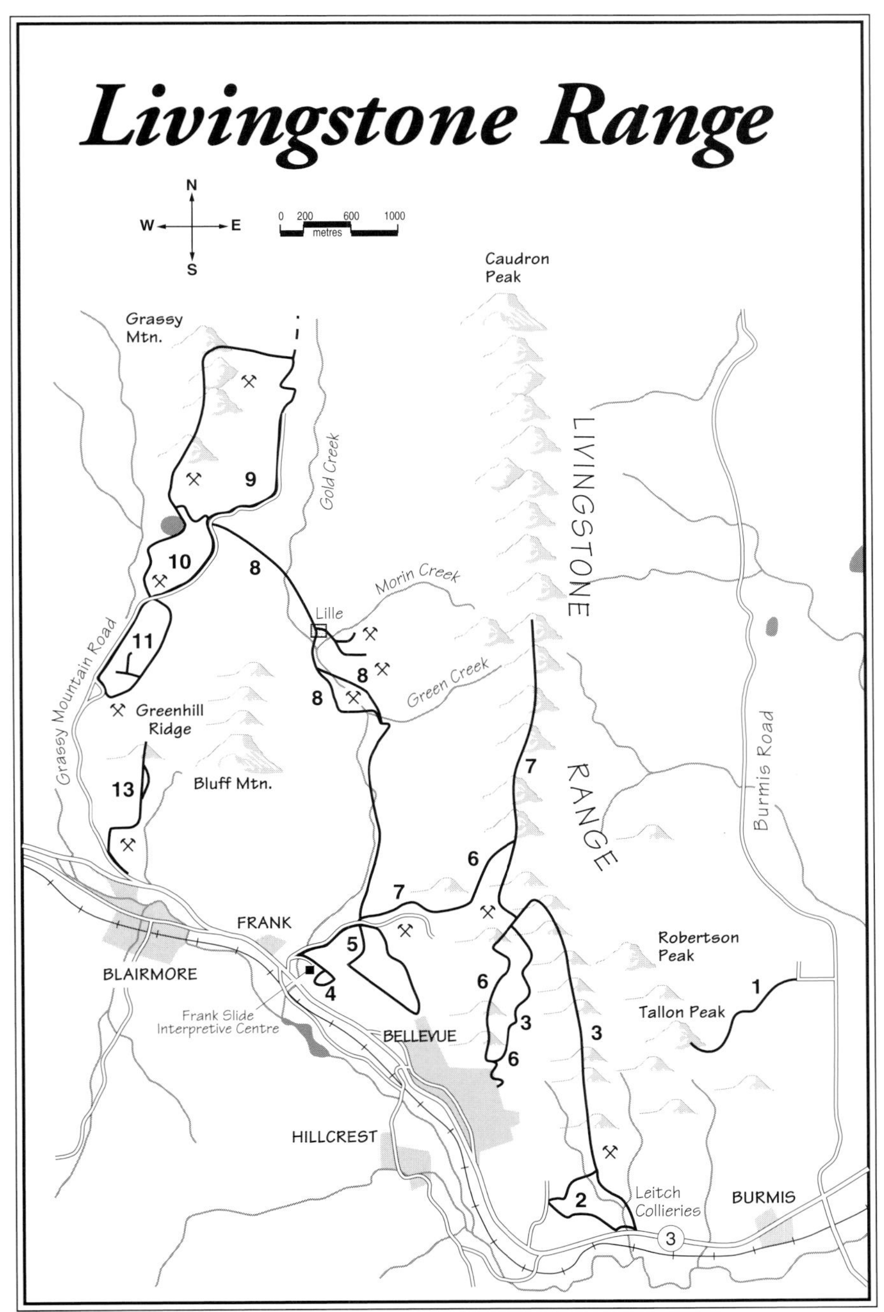
Livingstone Range
N
W
E
S
0 200 600 1000
metres
Caudron Peak
Grassy Mtn.
Gold Creek
9
10
8
Morin Creek
Lille
Green Creek
11
8
8
LIVINGSTONE RANGE
Grassy Mountain Road
Greenhill Ridge
Bluff Mtn.
13
7
Burmis Road
6
7
FRANK
5
BLAIRMORE
4
6
Robertson Peak
1
Tallon Peak
Frank Slide Interpretive Centre
3
3
BELLEVUE
6
HILLCREST
2
Leitch Collieries
BURMIS
3

# 1 TALLON PEAK

Tallon Peak is the highest point at the east end of the pass. Local people and visitors climb the mountain for its 360 degree panorama that takes in both the prairies to the east and the Flatheads and High Rock Range to the west. The elevation gain makes this a stiffer climb than would appear from the trailhead.

From the trailhead, climb over the fence running along the field to the left and walk uphill toward Tallon Peak. Within a short distance there are two other fences to climb over. If the aspen/poplar grove located between the second and third fence is wet early in the spring or after heavy rains, skirt the marshy ground by swinging to the left. After crossing the third fence, turn right onto an old road lined with forget-me-nots, shooting stars, dogtooth violets and crocus. At the next junction of several old trails, take the left-hand switchback leading uphill and over to the south flank of Tallon Peak. At a bench where the road disappears there are good views of the plains and foothills to the east and the Flatheads to the west. A pine grove in the lee of the shoulder makes a natural resting spot after the brisk climb.

**Duration** half day

**Distance** 5 km return

**Level of Difficulty** Moderately steep climb on unmarked trails.

**Maximum Elevation** 1814 m

**Elevation Gain** 457 m

**Map** Blairmore 82 G/9

## Access

Turn off Highway 3 at North Burmis Road and drive north for 3.8 km to a turnoff to the west. Continue for another 700 m down the gravel road and park your vehicle at a 90 degree turn in the road.

| | |
|---|---|
| 0 m | trailhead |
| 700 m | three fence crossings |
| 900 m | junction of several trails |
| 1.7 km | aspen grove |
| 2.0 km | fence |
| 2.5 km | peak |
| 5.0 km | return to trailhead |

*Prairie crocus.*

## Tallon Peak

The origin of the name of this mountain is somewhat confused. Some references suggest this 1814 m-high peak is named after L. Tallon, an assistant surveyor for the Canadian government who accompanied W. S. Drewry in his survey of the Rocky Mountains between 1888 and 1892. Residents of the Crowsnest Pass, though, state the spelling is incorrect as they feel the name is a descriptive one as the slope and the weathered ridges near the top of the mountain give the peak the profile of an eagle's talon.

*Tallon Peak.*

Refreshed, find the cattle trail that leads west up the slope. Several other cattle trails intersect; in all cases, bear to the right. The view directly in front is a delight, a beautiful contrast of wooded foothills and rugged mountains beyond. Once clear of the aspens, head straight up the steep slope that in spring is covered in wild sage. From here, Tallon Peak and the rock cairn marking its pinnacle are visible. Descend to a saddle, then climb to an open field and another aspen copse. Hike past the rock outcropping to another fence located farther up the slope. Fortunately, the slope is criss-crossed with game trails that make the ascent much easier. Once across this last fence, the way is clear to just below the summit where a rock face appears to be impregnable. Persevere. Skirt the cliff to the right and at a small break in the rock wall, scramble up to the highest point. Do not forget to add a rock to the cairn.

Return the way you came.

## Burmis

**Previous Name** Livingstone

A petition was sent to the federal government in 1906 to change the name of this railway whistle stop from Livingstone to a combination of the names of Robert H. Burns, a rancher living 13 km east, and Jack Kemmis, a rancher located outside of Cowley. Thus, Burmis became the official name of the nearby mining community.

Today, the number of homes and residents in the settlement at Burmis can be counted on one hand. A few small piles of coal slack, the remnants of an old mine-related grade possibly for a spur line between the mine and the Canadian Pacific Railway and a collapsed mine opening are all that remain of the on-again, off-again attempts by various investors to make the seams at Burmis profitable.

The first entrepreneur to cast his eyes on the seams at the east end of the Crowsnest Pass was American Samuel W. Gebo. Gebo came to the pass with an impressive list of coal mine developments in the United States and he hoped his endeavours at the railway siding known as Livingstone would pan out. In 1899, a year after the Canadian Pacific had completed its track through the pass, Gebo sunk a vertical shaft 148 m into the coal seams. But, as luck would have it, he encountered "dirty" coal that also showed signs of pinching out. Gebo pulled out and relocated to Turtle Mountain. The seams were not worked again until December 1907 when Peter Lund, a railway contractor who had opened a mine farther east at Lundbreck with John Breckenridge, began working "the old Livingstone shaft." Lund extracted 635 tonnes that year before ceasing operations. Poor markets and possibly poor coal were reasons cited by Lund to the provincial mine inspector.

Stronger markets enticed the Davenport Coal Company, backed by Spokane interests, to capitalize their Burmis holdings in 1909 at $500,000. Davenport successfully worked No. 2 and 5 seams until 1913. During its years of operation Davenport installed hoists to bring the coal to the surface, laid a spur line from the mine to the Canadian Pacific main line, constructed a timber tipple, a wash house for the miners, a blacksmith shop, a storehouse, a mine office, a lamp house and a Marcus screen to sort the coal into various sizes. Meanwhile, the company built 10 miners' cottages, a hotel and a barber shop. By 1914 Burmis boasted a population of 300. Capital expenditures were reflected in production, which rose from 9,851 tonnes in 1910 to 74,344 tonnes in 1913. But, the First World War and the loss of markets forced the demise of the Davenport concern and the closure of the mine. It was 10 years before another entrepreneur was willing to take a chance. Harold Rhodes, though, only worked the Burmis mine for two years. The seams at Burmis were worked sporadically by a number of small operators. Inferior coal had haunted the Burmis mine since the beginning and finally in 1962 the last of the operators at Burmis, C. & F. Mining, closed.

## Limber Pine

**Scientific Name** *Pinus flexilis*
**Other Names** Burmis Tree Rocky Mountain white pine

Next to Crowsnest and Turtle mountains, the Burmis tree is perhaps Crowsnest Pass' most recognizable landmark. Silhouetted against a backdrop of Turtle Mountain if travelling west or against a clear eastern sky, this 300 year-old limber pine has been photographed, painted and sketched numerous times.

Limber pine is a slow-growing, but long-lived species. The name "limber" is derived from the suppleness of the pine's young branches. Since limber pine prefers dry, exposed and windy rocky slopes and ridges, flexibility is key to its survival. Limber pines are often twisted and gnarled in appearance owing to the effects of the wind.

The Burmis tree died in 1978, but remained standing until October 1998 when it finally toppled from its sandstone outcrop next to Highway 3. The citizens of Crowsnest Pass spearheaded its restoration and local businesses, community groups and individuals worked with Historic Sites Service of the department of Community Development to restore the tree on its original location. The first attempt to prop up the tree failed; a drill bit broke when they tried to bore a hole up the trunk of the tree for a steel pipe. Finally, it was decided to bolt the exposed roots into the sandstone rock using large metal brackets.

*The Burmis tree.*

# 2 LEITCH COLLIERIES

The country at the east end of the Crowsnest Pass offers hikers the opportunity to reach open ridge tops with relative ease and to explore the ruins of various coal mines. This hike combines both, by looping above the Leitch Collieries mine workings, then exploring the surface plant, now a Provincial Historic Site. The walk ends with a visit to the site of the company town of Passburg.

Enter the cemetery and follow the track to the northeast corner. Climb over the fence, then head east across the flat meadow via an old wagon road. It dips to cross a stream, then passes through a fence opening. Keep to the right of the cattle feed stalls and go down toward the aspen grove. Here you bear to the right and go as far as the fence corner. You are now amongst the fan house and mine entry ruins of the Leitch Collieries.

To view the mine workings and to gain altitude for a sweeping vista of the pass, start climbing uphill on a poorly marked path that begins behind the bull pen. Bear slightly to the left when just above the mine entry. The objective is to get to the top of this hill. Once on top of the first hump, bear slightly to the right and climb to a fence and a rocky spine that you skirt on the left. The ridge above beckons, especially in the spring when the hillside is dotted with delicate shooting stars, crocus, pussytoes, violets and showy balsamroots. When

**Duration** half day
**Distance** 5.3 km return
**Level of Difficulty** Easy walk on four-wheel-drive tracks.
**Maximum Elevation** 1494 m
**Elevation Gain** 244 m
**Map** Blairmore 82 G/9

## Access

Drive 1.9 km west of Leitch Collieries Provincial Historic Site on Highway 3. At the entrance sign for the Municipality of Crowsnest Pass turn north onto a good gravel road and follow it for 1.2 km to a cemetery. Park here.

**Note**: The Leitch Collieries surface plant is a designated Provincial Historic Site and may not be disturbed.

| | |
|---|---|
| 0 m | cemetery |
| 400 m | stream |
| 1.0 km | remains of fan house |
| 1.3 km | fence |
| 1.6 km | slack piles and mine entrance |
| 2.0 km | ventilation shaft |
| 4.0 km | Leitch Collieries Provincial Historic Site |
| 5.3 km | trailhead |

*These foundation walls are all that remain of the town of Passburg.*

*Leitch Collieries Provincial Historic Site.*

the path enters a very small grove of spruce trees, head toward the closest rock outcropping to the left. Your destination is actually located above and farther to the left, but this is the easiest access. As you cross the low rocky outcropping, slack piles and a series of collapsed openings can be seen in front of you, offering a glimpse of what the mountain once looked like—a sharp contrast to the pleasant panorama of east Crowsnest Pass today.

From the slack piles it is a short but steep climb to a shoulder. Once there, two things become obvious: firstly, the top of the hill stretches out above you, and secondly, there are faint markings of an old wagon road leading toward the top. Located halfway along the road is a "lightning bolt" rock that shields hikers from the prevailing westerly winds that seem to blow constantly in this area. Continue up to where the track narrows through the spruce trees. Keep a sharp eye open to your left for an extremely dangerous air shaft beneath a rock outcropping. Approach with caution.

The route farther up the ridge is described under "Two Mine Trail," so from the shaft retrace your steps all the way down to the ruins of the fan house at the bottom of the hill. Turn left and follow either the old railbed that disappears twice where trestles once spanned the stream, or the old wagon road that runs parallel to it. This 670-m railbed connected the mine entries that you just visited to the tipple located at the site of the Leitch Collieries surface plant. Past a stream, the road forks. Take the left-hand fork. Both roadways lead to the Leitch Collieries Provincial Historic Site.

The historic site has a self-guided trail. Beginning at the stabilized stone structure of the power house, now *sans* roof, which used Leitch coal to fire the boilers that in turn produced the steam to run all the surface plant machinery, the path leads past the

## The Leitch Collieries

Leitch Collieries originally opened in 1907 south of Highway 3 near the confluence of Byron Creek and the Crowsnest River. But when the quality of coal there proved marginal, the mine managers opened No. 2 mine in 1909. An ambitious project for its Canadian backers, Leitch enjoyed only a few short years of operation. Nevertheless, in six years, Leitch miners extracted 430,000 tonnes of bituminous coal from the 2.5 m-thick seam.

On your way through the historic site you walked past the foundations of the tipple, the washery and at the extreme east end of the site a long low mound that represents 101 Mitchell coke ovens. The tipple was one of the most important of the surface plant structures for it was here that the coal was cleaned of rock and other debris by hand at a picking table. Once cleaned, it passed over a series of screens that separated the coal into different sizes from the largest pieces called lump, through nut and pea sizes to the finest coal pieces called slack. The slack was sent to the washery to be cleaned before being sent to the coking ovens. The Leitch washery was one of only two wet washeries ever to be built in the pass. In a wet washery, flotation separated and cleaned the coal from ash and other impurities. The cleaned slack was then dried before being sent to the coke ovens. Built from one million bricks by the first mine manager, Billy Hamilton, the ovens stretched the Leitch company to its financial limit. When overseas coke markets were lost with the outbreak of the First World War, Leitch was forced to close. The coke ovens remained, for Hamilton, "the regret of my life."

## A Frightening Ride

In addition to the cost of building a spur line, Leitch Collieries also had to build a shed over at least part of the track because of the very high winds that sometimes funnel through the pass. Today, the grade seems gentle enough. But there is a story that the grade and the speed of the train were too much for one inexperienced miner. So terrified did he become that he leapt from the coal car on which he was riding into the stream below. A broken leg and a bruised ego were his only rewards when he learned that the train had chugged to a controlled stop at the surface plant.

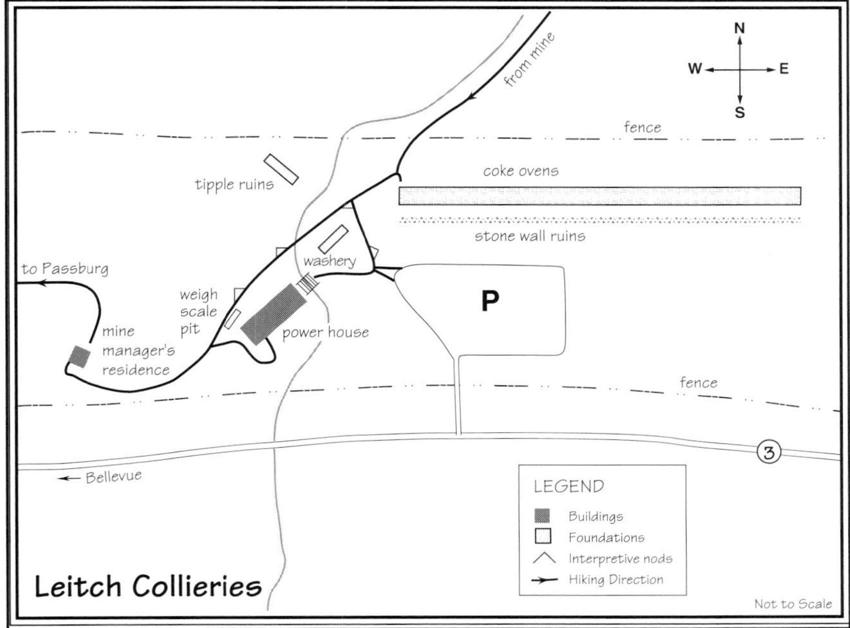


tipple, the washery and a row of 101 coke ovens. The walls of the once fine home of Billy Hamilton, the first mine manager at Leitch, are located at the west end of the site.

Associated with each mine was a town. In the case of Leitch Collieries, its town was Passburg, located just over the hill from Billy Hamilton's house. To visit "Passburg" and to return to your vehicle walk behind the mine manager's house and pick up the old road above. Follow the road as it climbs uphill and crosses a fence. At the top of the rise bear to the left to parallel Highway 3, continuing to follow the old wagon road to the concrete remains in the middle of a pasture. Passburg once boasted a grocery store, post office, butcher shop, bake shop, pool hall, a hotel, a school and a church. Several cellar depressions are noticeable on your way back through the field to the cemetery and your vehicle.

*Opposite: Leitch Collieries Ltd., ca. 1920. Courtesy Glenbow Archives, NA 2833-28.*

# 3 TWO MINE TRAIL

This hike offers something for everyone: a steep pull up to an unnamed ridge in the Livingstone Range for an unparalleled sight of mountains and prairie, and for those of you who enjoy poking around old ruins, some of the largest—and most dangerous—subsidence and ventilation shafts associated with two of the major mining companies in the pass, the Leitch Collieries and West Canadian Collieries.

At the trailhead bear to the right and pass through the barbed-wire gate, remembering to close it behind you. Walk up the old road. Approximately 200 m from the trailhead the road leads past a dilapidated log building and a "gingerbread" cottage tucked back into the trees. Shortly beyond this point, as you climb toward the ridge, there are several forks in the road. At the first fork bear to the right. Then just before a tumbled-down lumber building, keep to the left. At a third fork less than 1 km away turn right onto a road that begins to switchback steeply uphill with occasional views of the Frank Slide, Bellevue and Hillcrest. Once the road breaks out of the trees and onto the open slope, you are rewarded by a panoramic view of the whole valley. Look up and to the left and you

**Duration** day

**Distance** 9.8 km

**Level of Difficulty** First half up a steep pull up a hard-packed road. Then an easy ridge descent.

**Maximum Elevation** 2072 m

**Elevation Gain** 761 m

**Elevation Loss** 853 m

**Map** Blairmore 82 G/9

## Access

This hike necessitates two vehicles if you wish to avoid a long walk. Park your first vehicle at the Leitch Collieries site located on Highway 3. Then drive your second vehicle to the west end of 28 Ave. in Bellevue. At the top of the rise there is a turnabout area. This is your trailhead.

*Examining the well-crafted dovetail corners on the log outbuilding at the "gingerbread" cottage.*

will be able to see the remnants of an iron pulley hoist line just under the top of the ridge.

The road leads to a saddle. En route, at a fork in the road keep left. Scattered about on the other side of the saddle are mining relics from the heyday of West Canadian Collieries' Bellevue mine. Remnants of a hoist house and parts of cable lie strewn on the open slope. Do not continue to follow the road downhill (see "Iron Pulley Trail"). Instead, strike out for the top of the ridge to your right via a rough switchback path. The view from the top encompasses not only the by now familiar sight of Bellevue and Hillcrest below, but also, by looking in the opposite direction, the Livingstone Ridge marching to the north. Turn right and walk along the ridge. There is no real trail but the way is clear despite the rocky, rough underfooting. At a small cairn take a moment to add a rock and appreciate the 360 degree view of prairie and mountain.

*Crossing an interesting spine of rock.*

| | |
|---|---|
| 0 m | trailhead in Bellevue |
| 200 m | cottage |
| 900 m | first fork |
| 1.0 km | second fork |
| 1.8 km | third fork |
| 2.3 km | top of ridge |
| 2.8 km | cairn |
| 3.1 km | subsidence |
| 3.6 km | old road |
| 6.5 km | fence |
| 7.8 km | "lightning bolt" rock |
| 9.8 km | Leitch Collieries Provincial Historic Site |

Shortly beyond the cairn keep on the left side and scramble down a cliff to an old road. Subsidence holes created by the mining of the coal seam by West Canadian Collieries pockmark the ridge like huge craters. Be careful! The subsidence holes are open and are extremely dangerous. The old road is partially obscured by rocks and trees so it is a bit of a bushwhack along the subsidence to an open field at the end. Cut across the field to another old needle-strewn road that offers a very pleasant walk through open pine forest with views of Waterton Lakes National Park straight ahead. Wild sage covers the field where the road temporarily leaves the forest.

Where the road disappears, look for orange surveyor's tape that marks the pathway's descent. Once out of the forest and into parkland there is no real path at all, but the way down remains clear. Just

*View from high point of the trail looking toward Robertson Peak (left) and Tallon Peak (right).*

continue to follow the ridge as it swings to the east. Climb over a fence and continue down the ridge, following faint depressions of an old wagon road in the rocky soil. This section is also part of "Leitch Collieries" trail. The "road" leads past an open mine shaft part way down the slope. Unlike the previous subsidence holes, this shaft dates from a much earlier period of mining activity. In 1909, the Leitch Collieries, which had originally located south of the present-day Highway 3 on Byron Creek, moved lock, stock and barrel to Police Flats located almost directly below you. All equipment, materials and even houses were moved to the new mine site.

Farther down the road a large shattered rock makes a good resting spot. Views of both the east and the west ends of the pass can be enjoyed from this "lightning bolt" rock. Below the shoulder is a series of collapsed openings and subsidence associated with the Leitch mining operation. Swing to the left as you pick your way through the slack piles and cross a low spine of rock. Continue down and left to another rock outcropping. In the spring this entire slope is covered in shooting stars, balsamroot, violets and crocus, which are replaced in late summer by daisies and asters. Once through a grove of spruce trees, skirt another rock outcropping to the right. Cross the fence and swing slightly to the right. From the top of the final step, head left as you descend to the ruins of the Leitch fan house.

The old railbed and wagon road swing past the concrete platform located left of the ruins. Turn left and follow either one of these routes to Leitch Collieries Provincial Historic Site where your second vehicle is parked. If you have not done so already, take some time to take the self-guiding trail through the surface plant of the only fully Canadian-owned coal mine to have operated in the pass.

## Bellevue

"Quelle une belle vue!" Elise, the daughter of Jules Fleutot, the first managing director of West Canadian Collieries, exclaimed in 1903 when she looked across to the mountains from the level bench of land where the company had decided to build a town. Translating as "what a beautiful view," the name of Bellevue became official in 1905.

Lying just east of the Frank Slide on the north side of Highway 3 is the community of Bellevue. Like all communities in the Crowsnest Pass, Bellevue developed as a separate townsite. However, in January 1979, Bellevue along with all the other communities in the Crowsnest Pass was consolidated under one municipal government, the Municipality of Crowsnest Pass. Street names were one problem facing the new council. Almost every town had a "Main Street." In order to avoid duplication of names, the municipality opted to number all the streets and avenues. So, Bellevue's two original business streets, Front Street and Main Street, became 213 Street and 212 Street respectively; today, 213 Street is the main or west access off Highway 3 into town.

Like several other communities located at the east end of the pass, Bellevue was sited and developed by the French-based West Canadian Collieries. The coal mining company began its long history in the pass in 1898 when it began prospecting along Gold Creek, which led to the development of the seams at Lille. In 1904, a rich seam was discovered adjacent to the railway and the Bellevue townsite was laid out on a flat bench of land immediately above the mine. By 1905, 150 men were working at the Bellevue mine. Of all West Canadian Collieries' mines, the one at Bellevue dodged the cyclical market swings to close only in 1962 along with their Greenhill mine. Over its long history, the Bellevue mine produced more than one million tonnes of coal. If you wish to experience an underground coal mine, you can tour the Bellevue mine during the summer months. (See Useful Information: Tourist Attractions.)

The first 40 residences to house the men and their families were constructed in 1904. As the mine progressed, so too did the town. By 1917, Bellevue could claim a hotel, a drug store, a cafe, a pool room and cigar store, a livery stable and a refreshment parlour. All this was wiped out in a disastrous fire that swept through more than 20 buildings in the core of town in August 1917. After rebuilding along Front Street, the business section was levelled again three years later by another fire. As a consequence most of the buildings along 213 and 212 streets date from 1921. Normally a quiet town, Bellevue took on the hue of a "shoot 'em up" western town when, in 1920, three bank robbers were cornered in the Bellevue Cafe on 213 Street. (See Sentinel in High Rock Range Country chapter.)

Located farther east, along 27 and 28 avenues, is the old townsite of Maple Leaf. This small community was associated with the Maple Leaf mine that opened in 1907. Never large, Maple Leaf townsite nevertheless attracted a butcher, a shoemaker and a blacksmith to their community. Maple Leaf is now part of Bellevue.

*Bellevue, ca. 1910. Courtesy Glenbow Archives, NA 3903-1.*

# 4 THE FRANK SLIDE TRAIL

This is a rare opportunity to walk through one of the largest rock slides in the world that destroyed half the town of Frank and killed approximately 70 people. The Friends of the Frank Slide Interpretive Centre are responsible for this well-groomed path. It goes through the slide and along a portion of both the Frank and Grassy Mountain Railway and an old highway built to bypass the slide. An interpretive brochure linked to the 17 signposts along the trail explains the various features found.

From the trailhead, the path leads down the slope into the "splash" area of the Frank Slide. It's quite a sight. Straight in front is the dramatic scar of the slide on Turtle Mountain itself. But it is your immediate surroundings that catch most of your attention. Boulders as large as cars spread around and below you. Here and there you can see an odd spruce tree, but most of the scene is one of devastation. Along the way, keep an eye out for pikas and golden-mantled ground squirrels, two species normally found at much higher elevations. As you walk down the path you pass beneath the Frank Slide Interpretive Centre

**Duration** 1 hour
**Distance** 1400 m
**Level of Difficulty** Groomed trail.
**Maximum Elevation** 1402 m
**Elevation Loss** 30 m
**Map** Blairmore 82 G/9

## Access

Park at the Frank Slide Interpretive Centre 1.5 km north of Highway 3 near Frank. The trailhead, which is signed, is located at the east end of the parking lot.

*Opposite: Boulder from the Frank Slide ca. 1911. Courtesy Provincial Archives of Alberta, Archives Collection A 1771.*

*Walking along the trail through the slide.*

# The Frank Slide

In the early hours of April 29, 1903, without any warning, approximately 30,000,000 cu m of limestone broke off from the east face of Turtle Mountain, scooping everything in its path and crashing against the opposite side of the valley to a height of some 120-150 m. What could cause such a phenomenon? Miners at the Canadian-American Coal and Coke Company in Frank believed that mining and blasting weakened the mountain. Their assertion was echoed by William Pearce, mine inspector with the territorial government (Alberta did not become a province until 1905), who felt strongly that mining had weakened the mountain's internal structure to the point that the roof, weakened owing to robbing the pillars of too much coal, collapsed, thereby causing the slide. But Pearce's assumptions proved incorrect when survivors of the night shift reported that the tunnels and gangways were left largely intact after the slide. So, although mining might have been a contributing factor, it was not the basic cause. Certainly cracks had formed at the summit prior to the slide and perhaps the sequential freezing and thawing of water in the cracks caused the initial rocks to break loose. But probably the main cause of the slide was the geological structure of Turtle Mountain. The mountain is bisected by the Turtle Mountain Thrust Fault. Above the fault is hard limestone and below, softer layers of sandstone and shale. Folding of the rock layers has resulted in bedding planes on top of the mountain being tipped vertically with only a weak bonding holding the rock to the sharp angle of the bedding planes. Turtle Mountain, then, was top heavy. In addition, the Canadian-American Coal and Coke Company was mining coal seams embedded in the softer rocks at the mountain's base. Combined with the erosive action of the Crowsnest River, Turtle Mountain was a disaster waiting to happen.

Interestingly, the rock did not simply slide down the face of Turtle Mountain and across the valley. Shortly after the disaster, William Pearce noticed that portions of the slide had taken a nearly 180 degree turn and that some of the vegetation that had been on the top of the mountain had landed upright and had not been overturned. Probably the best explanation is

the air-layer lubrication theory. This states that when the slab of limestone first broke off from the mountain, it fell to a ridge that deflected the rocks up and over, thereby trapping air beneath the rocks and allowing them to "ride" to their present location. "Splash" rocks, riding on top of the slide, were thrown ahead. In only 100 seconds, the entrance and entire surface plant of the Canadian-American Coal and Coke Company located at the base of Turtle Mountain, a portion of the town of Frank, some 2133 m of the main line of the Canadian Pacific Railway and the lower portion of the Frank and Grassy Mountain Railway were buried. The average depth of the slide is 14 m, although in places boulders lie 30 m deep. Some 2.5 sq. km of valley floor are covered in a blanket of limestone boulders, the largest of which weighs 5.5 million kilograms!

## The Aftermath

A few people in Frank were already awake on that fateful morning. Hearing a loud noise that they mistakenly took for an explosion or that of steam escaping under high pressure, they rushed outside thinking that a disaster had happened at the mine. Instead, dust and boulders the size of rail cars swept past their doors. Some eyewitnesses claimed they saw rock hurl itself against a terrace opposite Turtle Mountain, then fall back to the floor of the valley. Others who had been asleep awakened to find themselves miraculously alive. Mr. Warrington felt his house shake and the next thing he knew he had been flung 12 m amongst the boulders. Lester Ackroyd woke up underneath what had been his home and escaped through a hole between the rocks. He staggered to a friend's house where he collapsed owing to a punctured spleen. Syd Choquette, a brakeman and uninjured, knew that a passenger train was due shortly. With little regard for himself, he climbed over boulders slippery with rock dust to flag down the approaching train. For his bravery, he was promised a lifetime job with Canadian Pacific Railway. For the survivors, it was a disaster that passed all comprehension and by the time a detachment of the North West Mounted Police arrived the next day, no one was sober! Fearing another landslide, Pearce ordered the evacuation of the town. A canvas city was set up to house the residents, the injured being taken by special train to a police detachment building just west of the townsite. Communication lines between Blairmore and communities farther west and Burmis and beyond to the east had been cut off. The Canadian Pacific rushed men and supplies to the disaster area and completed new rail- and telegraph lines through the slide in record time. It took considerably longer—three years—to reconstruct a wagon road through the slide.

and through a green oasis that escaped the slide. An interpretive signpost informs you when you reach the old railbed of the Frank and Grassy Mountain Railway. Farther along, at signpost #15, there is a 90 degree turn in the path that takes you along the old highway, rebuilt after the slide wiped out the original wagon road connecting the Crowsnest Pass with the plains to the east. From here the path leads up a steep hill, bringing you back to the parking lot and your vehicle.

**Note**: The Frank Slide is a designated Provincial Historic Site and may not be disturbed.

| | |
|---|---|
| 0 m | trailhead |
| 600 m | signpost #9 |
| 1.1 km | signpost #15 |
| 1.4 km | parking lot |

# 5 SKIRTING THE SLIDE—THE BELLEVUE MINE

Looping from the Frank Slide Interpretive Centre to Bellevue and back, this easy hike introduces you to the West Canadian Collieries' Bellevue mining operation. For most of the hike Turtle Mountain and the Frank Slide serve as dramatic backdrops.

From the centre, retrace your steps down the access road. At the switchback in the paved road there is a gravel road turning off to the right. Follow it uphill for 2 km to a junction. Turn right onto a rough road that proves too difficult for even four-wheel-drive vehicles. A short distance along, bear right onto a hiking path that weaves through the pine forest, affording constant views of the Frank Slide. It returns to the road at several points until it reaches a building foundation. A short distance past the foundation, an old grassy road leads to the right from the rough road and is littered with coal slack indicating a mine is nearby. The barbed-wire fence at the edge of the ridge protects the unwary from a large, nasty subsidence above the underground West Canadian Collieries' Bellevue mine.

The grassy road soon forks. The right-hand fork leads to another barbed-wire fence surrounding a mine opening and subsidence. The left fork leads past small slack piles, then back to the rough road where you turn right. Almost immediately there is a cattleguard and a fork. Keep to the right on the road that descends the hill to Bellevue's water cistern and Firemen's Park. Steps lead up from the park to a pleasant ridge overlooking the town. Typical of mining towns at the turn of the 20th century, Bellevue has a residential area that sports neat miners' cottages. Most are one storey, wood frame buildings with clapboard or vinyl siding.

To return, follow the hydro line toward the Frank Slide Interpretive Centre. Interspersed with pine and spruce trees, the open ridge makes a very pleasant walk. Part way along, turn right onto another old road that leads back to a gravel road. Here, bear left and go down the hill to the paved road that leads back up the hill to the Frank Slide Interpretive Centre.

**Duration** half day

**Distance** 7.8 km return

**Level of Difficulty** Easy walk on four-wheel-drive road. Return route follows hydro line.

**Maximum Elevation** 1372 m

**Elevation Gain** 61 m

**Map** Blairmore 82 G/9

## Access

Park your vehicle at the Frank Slide Interpretive Centre 1.5 km north of Highway 3 near Frank.

| | |
|---|---|
| 0 m | Frank Slide Interpretive Centre parking lot |
| 0.5 km | junction of gravel road |
| 2.4 km | junction of road |
| 3.9 km | Bellevue mine site |
| 4.3 km | community park |
| 7.8 km | return to parking lot |

## The Bellevue Mine

West Canadian Collieries' Bellevue mine, opened in 1903, was the second coal mine begun by the company. It had first opened the Lille mines to the north and later bought and leased land that included Blairmore to the west and Adanac Ridge on the south. The coal company began exploiting the 3.5 m-thick seam at Bellevue in 1904 and by the following year had 150 men working the mine. Production rose quickly. In 1907, the Bellevue mine was producing 1200 tonnes of coal daily, reaching its top production in the years 1925 to 1929 when the figure rose to some 2500 tonnes. Over its nearly 60 year history about 1,364,000 tonnes of bituminous coal were taken out of the ridge. Along with the company's Greenhill mine, the Bellevue seams kept the company competitive until 1962 when the French-based company was forced to close owing to shrunken markets.

## Gas Explosion!

Poking around subsidence such as that found along this hike can be dangerous. But not as dangerous as it was to work in the gaseous mines of the Crowsnest Pass. Lethal methane gas constantly escaped from the coal face. Experienced miners knew the methane "moved" the coal and they learned to use the gas to help "work" the coal. However, they also knew how potentially dangerous methane gas could be. Lighter than air, methane collected in pockets at the roof of the rooms where the miners worked. If the concentration of methane was too high, it could trigger an explosion when combined with either dust that tended to hang in the air from mining or from rock falls from the roof. The miners, then, worked in a continuously precarious situation.

Alberta's first mine disaster struck the Bellevue mine on December 9, 1910, when gas exploded and ripped through the underground workings. Of the 47 miners who went into the mine that day only 17 emerged. The mine superintendent, Jack Powell, rushed to shut down the fans that were forcing the afterdamp deeper into the mine. Afterdamp is a mixture of carbon monoxide and carbon dioxide that is always released after a methane gas explosion. There was no mine rescue team in the pass at the time and one had to be sent for from Hosmer, B.C. Meanwhile, Powell and others without thought of their own safety rushed into the mine. By the time the mine rescue team arrived Powell and others had helped 17 survivors to the surface and had recovered 19 bodies of their mates. Equipped with proper breathing apparatus, the rescue team descended into the mine in the hope of finding more survivors and to recover any more bodies. The bodies of some miners were discovered near a fresh air outlet where they had congregated in the vain hope of escaping the deadly afterdamp. But the terror for families, the rescue team and any miners still alive underground was not over. A cave-in later that same day triggered the release of more afterdamp. The rescue team itself had to be rescued when many were overcome by the gas and one rescue worker, Fred Alderson, did not make it to the surface alive. The 31 miners who died were mourned by families and miners from Bellevue and other pass mines at the burial service held in Blairmore on 13 December.

*At the coal face, ca. 1951. Courtesy Provincial Archives of Alberta, Archives Collection A 9928.*

*Underground slump, August 1951. Courtesy Provincial Archives of Alberta, Public Affairs Bureau Collection PA 1984/1.*

# 6 IRON PULLEY TRAIL

A stunning view of prairies and mountains is just one reward awaiting you from a windswept ridge top. Interest is perked by visits en route to a fan house, a hoist house and the remains of the hoist system associated with Maple Leaf mines initially and later with Hillcrest Mohawk mines.

From your second vehicle, walk along the four-wheel-drive track for 100 m to a long open cut made for an underground gas line. Follow the cut uphill. On your right you will notice a wooden flume at the edge of the cut and from the top of the first rise a trail leading down to it.

At the top of the rise is a road allowance leading down to the right. If you follow the road, you will see a rather indistinct path opposite a coal slack pile. The path leads up a narrow ravine to a ventilation shaft and a fan house with the fan still intact. It is not often you have the opportunity to view such objects at close range and it helps to understand both the amount and the force of air that was being driven underground for the benefit of the miners. From the fan house a path heads up and to the right to two mine openings. You can still feel the rush of air escaping from one of the openings. But do not attempt a closer look. Mine openings are dangerous! The fan house, foundation and openings were owned by West Canadian Collieries for their Bellevue mine.

Once you have finished exploring, follow the old road down the hill to the road allowance and hence back to the cutline.

Now climb the track along the pipeline cut to a saddle on the main spine of the Livingstone Range. En route, the "Along the Livingstone Ridge" hike turns off to the left from a steep switchback close to the TransAlta tower. The switchback offers a magnificent view of the prairies to the northeast and the Rockies to the southwest. The wild chives can be found among the wildflowers sprinkling the open hillsides.

**Duration** half day

**Distance** 9.0 km

**Level of Difficulty** A steep climb on four-wheel-drive road to an open ridge. Option ridge or road descent.

**Maximum Elevation** 1799 m

**Elevation Gain** 427 m

**Elevation Loss** 488 m

**Map** Blairmore 82 G/9

## Access

To avoid a long walk, you require two vehicles. Park your first vehicle on the west extension of 28 Ave. in Bellevue. To access the trailhead where you will park your second vehicle, follow the access road from Highway 3 to the Frank Slide Interpretive Centre. Where the road forks, keep straight ahead, cross the cattleguard and continue up the gravel road for 1.6 km. Park your vehicle at the junction with the four-wheel-drive track on the left.

| | |
|---|---|
| 0 m | trailhead |
| 300 m | fan house and mine openings |
| 1.4 km | bottom of Livingstone Range |
| 3.2 km | hoist house on road descent |
| 4.0 km | first fork |
| 4.8 km | second and third forks |
| 4.9 km | fourth fork |
| 5.8 km | 28 Ave. Bellevue |

*Opposite: Ruins of the fan house near the beginning of the trail.*

From the saddle and tower head southeast along a game trail. Constant views to the right of the Rockies, the Frank Slide and the towns of Blair–more, Bellevue and Hillcrest accompany you. At a major clearing the trail joins an old vehicle road that leads to a West Canadian Collieries' hoist house made of concrete and hollow red brick, the company's building material trademark. Hoist houses were associated with a mine's haulage system of bringing the coal to the surface. Early mines used either horses or hoists to move the coal cars from the entry to the furthermost point along the main gangway. Farther up the slope from the hoist house you will notice the remains of a wooden pulley system and a mine opening. Follow the road to a saddle on the ridge where there is a choice of routes down the hill to your first vehicle.

**Option A—Road Descent**: This is the "Two Mine Trail" hike in reverse. Descend by walking along the road that leads down to your left. At a fork at the first switchback bear right, remaining on the primary road. If you happen to be here in August, this stretch offers a feast of wild rasp–berries from bushes lining the entire west side of the road. By looking up to your right you will be able to see just under the ridge top the remnants of an iron pulley hoist line.

The road continues to switchback steeply downhill with open views across to the Frank Slide, Bellevue and Hillcrest. A second fork in the road dictates a left turn in order to continue descending. Located just past a tumble-down lumber building is a third fork. Keep right. At yet a fourth fork go left and continue to descend. A charming "gingerbread" cottage with several log outbuildings are located a mere 200 m from your first vehicle.

**Option B—Ridge Descent**: The more adventurous should turn right and follow a path south from the saddle through a stand of pines. Downslope to the right are stockpiled mine timbers, shaft openings and subsidence. At the end of the ridge

you break out of the pines onto an open slope. Follow a line of subsidence down a rocky ridge, remembering that subsidence openings can be dangerous, so exercise caution. You will notice that an abandoned pulley system along the route includes a large iron pulley for which this trail is named.

At the end of the ridge scramble down the slope to a narrow ravine with a pleasant stream lined on one side by moss-covered stones and on the other by a drystone retaining wall marking the end of a road that led to this site. Follow the road. Once out of the ravine, the roadbed becomes obvious and in its descent switch–backs a few times. Cross a cattle–guard. Bear sharply to the right at a crossroads, following the switch–backs in the road to a junction of several roads. Keep to the right. You are now only 1 km from your pick-up vehicle.

*Dangerous surface subsidence on descent to Bellevue.*

## Wild Chives

**Scientific Name** *Allium schoenoprasum*

This common plant can be found from low elevations to the treeline, along riverbanks to rocky slopes. Its distinctive oniony smell and its purple round flowerheads distinguish it from the poisonous white camas.

The chives you grow in your garden are derived from this plant. Slender, hollow leaves narrow to a tip at the end of the stem. In June and July its densely-clustered, tuft-like purple inflorescences can be seen from a distance nodding in the breezes.

Like its domestic cousin, the entire plant is edible. The strongest and hottest flavour comes from the purplish bulb. But if you desire a more delicate flavour in a garnish or in any number of dishes, use the leaves. Because wild chives contain less sulphur than the domestic variety, they are more easily digested. The plant also has a number of medicinal attributes from lowering "bad" cholesterol to stopping vomiting.

# 7 ALONG THE LIVINGSTONE RIDGE

A good hike for those of you who yearn for open slopes and high ridges, this tramp along the spine of the Livingstone Range south of Caudron Peak to a minor summit offers truly wonderful views. A combination of significant elevation gain and an exposed ridge with brisk breezes means that at least two litres of water should be carried on warm days.

Walk along the four-wheel-drive track for 100 m to a long, open cut made for an underground gas line. Follow the cut uphill as far as the base of the Livingstone Range. The lower slopes are composed of a series of benches or steps. On your right you will notice a wooden flume at the edge of the cut and from the top of the first rise a trail leading down to it. At the top of this rise is a road leading down to the right. Unless you wish to explore some mine workings described in "Iron Pulley Trail," continue uphill on the cutline.

**Duration** day

**Distance** 12.6 km return

**Level of Difficulty** Moderate ridge walk with significant elevation gain. Four-wheel-drive road, open ridge and scree.

**Maximum Elevation** 2194 m

**Elevation Gain** 671 m

**Map** Blairmore 82 G/9

## Access

Take the access road from Highway 3 leading to the Frank Slide Interpretive Centre. Where the road forks keep straight ahead, cross the cattleguard and continue up the gravel road for 1.6 km. Park your vehicle at the junction with the four-wheel-drive track on the left.

| | |
|---|---|
| 0 m | trailhead |
| 1.1 km | bottom of the Livingstone Range |
| 2.0 km | top of the ridge |
| 4.0 km | saddle overlooking Green Creek |
| 6.3 km | rock cairn |
| 12.6 km | return to trailhead |

*View looking west from the ridge.*

Join a four-wheel-drive road heading up to a TransAlta tower on a saddle. Leave the road at the switchback close to the tower and bear left, climbing up to a rocky ridge top. On the way watch for purple wild bergamots, silky lupines, purple wild chives and pretty yellow mountain meadow cinquefoils.

Once on top, follow the ridge for approximately 4 km on its march north. There is no defined path but it is not needed as the route is obvious. Wonderful views to the right of the prairie and to the left of Turtle Mountain accompany you for the entire climb. Some scree makes footing a little uneven, so watch your step. En route are clumps of "krummholz," wind-deformed aspen and spruce trees, low bush cranberry and juniper.

At the first of a series of rocky promontories, follow a flower-strewn meadow to the right toward a continuation of the ridge. Ahead is a rock formation called a dragon's back. As you approach it, you will see a game trail to the right leading between two of the spines. Here, you are greeted by a magnificent view of your destination. Coming off the dragon's back you find yourself on a flat grassy saddle above Green Creek.

Next, search for a faint trail to the left of the ridge that parallels the spine and leads to the base of the final ridge. In front is a long scree slope showing a distinct path. It is a steep pull but you are inspired to continue as better and better views of Highway 22 and ranching country to the right and of grey rock faces of summits farther along the ridge straight ahead come into sight. A cairn at an unnamed summit between Green and Morin creeks marks the end of the trail.

Return the way you came.

*Adding a rock to the cairn.*

## Ancient Quarries

Would it surprise you to learn that prehistoric man quarried this exposed limestone ridge? In fact, there are a series of ancient quarries along the ridge where prehistoric peoples roughed out tools from chert, a form of quartz found as nodules in the limestone. Rather than haul the quarried chert all the way down to their campsites, the workers stayed at the quarries and roughly shaped the chert into "blanks," so-called because their final form and function had not yet been determined. Once back at their campsite, the workers may have completed the tool-making process, or they may have chosen to carry the blanks with them to be worked later, when needed.

In roughing out the blanks, the prehistoric peoples left behind literally thousands of flakes of waste rock scattered along the ridge.

## Livingstone Range

When you first approach the Crowsnest Pass from the east along Highway 3, the most impressive sight you notice is the wall of the Livingstone Range rising abruptly above the plain. This sharp change of typography between prairie and mountain demarcates the Livingstone Fault. In the mountain-building process the rocks were under tremendous pressure. When this pressure overcame the strength of the rocks, they fractured and slid past one another forming a fault. There are several types of faults, but the most important one here is the thrust fault. As tremendous pressure was exerted from the west, rocks fractured and slid eastward overriding younger formations. The result was that older formations often formed the tops of mountains while the younger formations are at the base. The Livingstone Thrust Fault has older limestones pushed over younger sandstones.

Exploring these limestone rocks will keep fossil hunters happy for hours. As most of the limestone rock in the pass was formed some 300 million years ago in a warm, shallow sea, small marine fossils such as brachiopods (lamp shells) can be found in large numbers. Other common fossils include crinoid stems and various types of bryozoans, which can be identified by their lacy pattern.

Lieutenant Thomas Blakiston was a magnetic observer attached to the Palliser Expedition (1857-1860), the purpose of which was to explore much of the Canadian prairies from the Red River to the Rockies. Blakiston named this impressive range after Dr. David Livingstone, best known for his explorations in Africa in the 19th century.

# 8 LILLE

There is always something fascinating about ghost towns and ghostly ruins. This is especially true of Lille, situated as it is 7 km north of the pass in the heart of the mountains. Its silent remains underscore the gamble taken by the early mining entrepreneurs. A walk up to Lille along the railbed of the Frank and Grassy Mountain Railway and visits to all three mine sites give you a sense of the size of the gamble that West Canadian Collieries took—and lost.

From your trailhead return to the main gravel road. Turn left and continue to walk along this hard-packed road as it winds its way toward Lille. The walk into Lille along the road is somewhat tedious especially as you can drive most of the way. However, after visiting Lille, you return to your vehicle via a combination of the old cart track that connected Lille with Frank and the railbed of the Frank and Grassy Mountain Railway. We think it is better to get the tedium out of the way at the beginning of the day so that you can enjoy your visit to Lille and your tramp down the valley.

**Duration** day

**Distance** 14.2 km return

**Level of Difficulty** An easy walk to and around Lille. Easy, well-blazed trail to No. 1 mine. Bushwhacking with some routefinding problems on lower portion of Frank and Grassy Mountain Railway.

**Maximum Elevation** 1585 m

**Elevation Gain** 244 m

**Map** Blairmore 82 G/9

## Access

Take the access road from Highway 3 leading to the Frank Slide Interpretive Centre. Where the road forks, keep straight ahead, cross a cattleguard and continue up the gravel road for 1.6 km. Park at the junction with a four-wheel-drive track to the left.

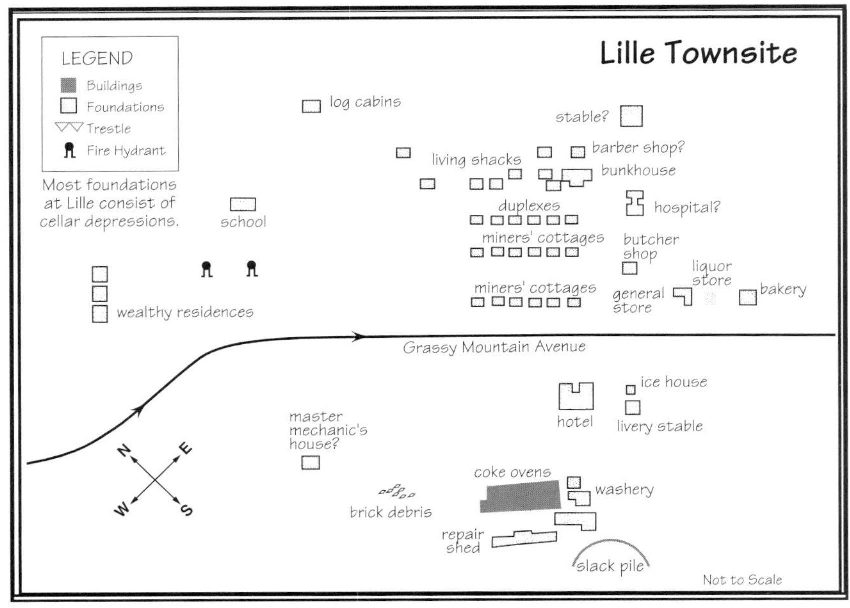

It is a straightforward walk up the road as far as a footbridge over Gold Creek. Walk up the hill under the TransAlta transmission line. From the tower it is a 2 km walk along a four-wheel-drive road into Lille. At one point, on the left where the road reenters mixed forest just before you reach the Lille townsite, there is a blazed tree marking the spot where you can cut through the bush for less than 25 m to the overgrown Lille cemetery. There are only a few unmarked headstones and wooden crosses left, but depressions can be found nearby. Little is known about the cemetery; it seems to have been used for only a short time. Continue on the road. Jump across Gold Creek and within a short distance you break out onto a wide meadow that once was the townsite of Lille.

*Headstone, Lille cemetery.*

At first, it appears as though little remains of the first West Canadian Collieries town. To your right you can find depressions in the ground where there was once a bakery and general store. Other depressions and foundations are scattered throughout the field where once miners' cottages, an ice house and livery stable that housed the mine horses and even fire hydrants stood. The remnants of the brick schoolhouse can be found at the far end of the field to the northeast. Most visible of all the ruins is the stone foundation walls of the hotel, located to the left of the track that bisects the townsite. Before visiting the hotel ruins and the surface plant remains, short detours to two of the mines are well worth the extra time.

No. 3 mine was the smallest of the operating mines. To access the mine opening and its debris, turn right onto a track opposite the hotel ruins that leads north through the field. Hop across Morin Creek. After the track switchbacks there is a junction at the top of the rise. Take the left-hand fork or the one that leads straight ahead and

**Note**: Lille is a designated Provincial Historic Site and may not be disturbed.

| | |
|---|---|
| 0 m | trailhead |
| 2.4 km | cemetery |
| 3.0 km | Lille |
| 3.5 km | No. 2 mine |
| 4.2 km | coke ovens |
| 4.8 km | waterfalls |
| 5.7 km | fan house |
| 7.0 km | No. 1 mine |
| 7.2 km | Green Creek and trail |
| 7.6 km | waterfall |
| 8.2 km | Frank and Grassy Mtn. railbed |
| 8.8 km | bridge |
| 10.2 km | trestle |
| 12.1 km | cart trail |
| 13.8 km | road |
| 14.2 km | trailhead |

The washery today.

continue for approximately 400 m to a second poorly marked fork. If you look sharply to the left just beyond the fork, you can see coal slack down the slope and through the thick trees. A bushwhack down the slope and across Morin Creek leads to the mine. After exploring the site return to the four-wheel-drive track.

To visit No. 2 mine, the largest producer of the Lille mines, return to the first fork and turn left, climbing uphill to a junction with an old road. Follow the road to the right. It passes mine adits or openings and winds around a rock face, eventually widening into a roadbed and crossing under the TransAlta power lines. Ignore an old road that joins in from the left and continue straight ahead to the mine site. Look for remains of coal cars, a boiler foundation and a pressure pipe to your right and down the slope. Near the bottom of the slope you can find three mine entrances and another two near the top of the hill. Except for the smallest operations, the mining companies always dug more than one entry. The main entry was paralleled by a counter entry and if the seam was large enough, as appears to have been the case with that of No. 2 mine, more counter entries were dug.

On a hot day a rest in the grove of trees adjacent to the little pond makes a pleasant break.

If you wish to gain a little altitude and a viewpoint over Lille, return to the road that joined the main trail immediately before No. 2 mine site. It leads uphill. At a fork in the road, bear left to gain access to the viewpoint. From here, the entire Lille townsite is laid out before you.

Return to the townsite the same way you came up. Cross the four-wheel-drive track that brought you into Lille and walk over to the stone foundation of the hotel. A fence now surrounds the hotel ruins but you can walk along the fence line down to the front of the building. To access the remains of the surface plant follow the cart trail that leads down from the hotel. In summer, the ruins of the surface plant are hidden by trees. Entry to the site can be gained through a gate in the fence erected by the leaseholder to protect both his cattle and the historic structures. Inside the fence are ruins of coke ovens built in 1903, a washery constructed in 1906-07 and a repair shed. Behind these remains, you can see a huge pile of coal slack.

Even in ruins, the row of 50 Bernard coke ovens is impressive. Lille was not the only mine that engaged in the expense of constructing coke ovens to convert slack coal to coke. Coke for the smelters of southeast British Columbia was a promising market in the first decade of the 20th century. Lorries ran along the top of the ovens and dumped slack coal into each oven, which was then closed and heated to extremely high temperatures until all gases had been removed. The result was coke, a fuel that burns so hot it can melt metal. Once the coking process was completed, the oven doors were removed and the coke spread onto the wharf to cool. Then it was shovelled into coal cars on the track below. Because so much remains of these ovens, it does not take a great deal of imagination to appreciate the sights, sounds and acrid smell of the coking operation. By searching the wharf and the area adjacent to the coke ovens, you might be able to find some coke that looks a little like coal but is very porous and light in weight. As you are poking about the coke ovens, examine the individual bricks of the ovens and you will notice that each has a stamp with a number. The ovens were prefabricated in Belgium and the numbers on each brick allowed for easy reassembly at Lille. Do not remove any bricks or coke from the site; Lille is a designated Provincial Historic Site and protected through the Historic Resources Act. By removing any material you could

*Pulling coke from the ovens at Lille mines, 1908. Courtesy Provincial Archives of Alberta, Archives Collection A 11025.*

*The coke ovens today.*

be prosecuted for damaging the historic integrity of the site.

To the left of the coke ovens are the foundations of the washery. Before small-sized slack coal could be converted into coke, it had to be washed. Here as much ash and rock as possible were removed through flotation. The lighter, clean coal floated and the ash sank. Cleaning the coal was important because smelting companies would not pay as much for dirty coke.

In order to visit No. 1 mine and to return to your vehicle, follow a well-blazed trail along the railbed of the Frank and Grassy Mountain Railway from the coke ovens down to Gold Creek. In several places the impressions of rail ties are still visible. In less than 1 km is located a pretty waterfall and shortly beyond a knee-high ford across Gold Creek. On the other side, continue to follow the blazed trail as it hugs the creek.

Shortly after bisecting a four-wheel-drive track (the historic cart track to Lille from the south), the blazed trail leads back to the stream that you have to ford again. Climb the slope, following a cattle trail. At the top of the bank, continue along cattle trails that head downstream, paralleling the creek below. Soon the ruins of the power house at the No. 1 mine become visible. Stay on the cattle trail as it leaves the open field and passes through poplar bush.

Before visiting the surface plant, a side trip to a fan house at the top of a hill is worthwhile. After two small clearings, the trail crosses a larger meadow with a row of spruce trees along the left-hand edge. Cross the opening and climb the hill, being careful to avoid the subsidence holes that are always an indication that you are walking on top of an old mine. Bear to the left and follow a faint trail through more spruce. Just beyond and above the slack pile is the fan house and ventilation shaft that were necessary to all mines. This makes a natural resting spot before continuing.

Retrace your steps to the cattle trail in the meadow, turn left and descend through woodlands. The trail crosses a small stream and then forks. Turn right. At the top of a small knoll is a substantial slack pile and a very dangerous open mine shaft. Do not attempt a closer look! The trail continues through the woods to another slack pile. Here, cross Green Creek to access the four-wheel-drive track (now the TransAlta road) on the other bank. Turn right and follow the road downhill across a log bridge. Just before the bridge over Gold Creek, an old roadbed to the right leads to the No. 1 mine.

Perched on the edge of Gold Creek are the remains of the stone power house built in 1906 or 1907 and accessed by a gate in the fence. Power houses were among the very first buildings to be constructed at a mine because they supplied all the power for the tipple machinery, the ventilation fans, haulage systems, and in this case, power of the town of Lille. Coal-fired boilers produced steam that fed steam engines that supplied the power to operate all the equipment supporting the under–ground operation. The engineers responsible for the smooth operation of the power house were paid less than the miners, but unlike the miners were never out of work.

The first work done at any mine site was the clearing of the bush and the digging out and timbering of the main gangway. To locate No. 1's mine opening, follow the little rivulet by the ruins of the power house up to the collapsed mine entrance. Many mines have underground streams. Miners, however, did not appreciate a wet workplace and demanded extra pay. The mining companies agreed, based on their definition of "wet:" if enough water dripped from the roof of the mine to soak a man's clothing or if the miner had to stand in enough water to soak his clothing above the knees, it could be considered a wet workplace!

*Power house for Lille No. 1 mine, 1906. Courtesy Glenbow Archives, NA 3903-110.*

Return to the TransAlta road. Turn left and walk uphill to recross the bridge over Gold Creek.

Immediately past the bridge turn right onto a distinct trail leading up to and under the TransAlta power line. Fifty metres beyond the powerline the trail forks. Bear right and climb up to a meadow where you swing right toward Gold Creek. At the end of the meadow and to the left are two trails. Take the one on the right that descends toward the creek. This part of the trail was the old cart trail that paralleled the railway from Lille down to Frank. Most people wanting to visit other towns in the pass used the cart trail instead of the railway. At the edge of the bank overlooking Gold Creek turn left and follow the ridge downstream until the sound of a waterfall becomes quite distinct. To view this beautiful three-tiered waterfall and the Gold Creek gorge, scramble down the bank as far as possible. Although the slope is steep, it makes a pleasant resting spot.

Return to the trail that now circles uphill following the ridge. Trails diverge, but all start to descend while continuing to follow the creek. Eventually, the trail emerges onto a meadow and crosses a fence lying on the ground. Look below: trestle timbers and a rail still embedded in the cliff opposite speak of the Frank and Grassy Mountain rail line that once connected Lille to the Crowsnest Pass. From here, bushwhack into a very narrow ravine and climb up the opposite ridge. Just below is a bench that is the railbed. Scramble down the slope to trestle timbers marking an unknown part of the workings along the line.

Follow the creek to a log bridge and cross it. After the stream has been on your left for approximately 100 m recross the stream just above a small cascade. There is no bridge at this second crossing and the water is cold. Climb up the slope and relocate the railbed that you now follow until it obviously disappears where once it

*Ruins of power house, Lille No. 1 mine, ca. 1990.*

The ruins of the power house on the eve of the millennium.

was trestled across Gold Creek. From here, follow a game trail down to the creek and bushwhack along the east bank. After a short distance, the tail climbs high above the creek to an open slope and skirts around to the next hill. Bushwhack down the slope to the forest where game trails lead you through the woods. Do not attempt to gain access to the creek at this point, as it was in this area that the Frank and Grassy Mountain Railway crossed and recrossed Gold Creek numerous times. Instead, find game trails about halfway up the slope. At some point, they all begin to lead down the slope, which has become much more gentle. Use any one to bring you back to the Frank and Grassy Mountain railbed. From here it is a straightforward hike down the railbed. Unfortunately, the bed is overgrown with shrubs and evergreens that make this part of the hike no easier than the sections farther upstream. At two spots where the railbed disappears at dips where there used to be trestles, follow connecting trails. Shortly after the last trestle, the railbed leads out to the old cart trail. It is now only a short distance to your vehicle.

## The Frank and Grassy Mountain Railway

The Frank and Grassy Mountain Railway was built in 1901 to transport coal and coke from the Lille mines to the main line of the Canadian Pacific Railway and then to market. Its 11 km-long line was built at great expense to its owners, West Canadian Collieries. A number of switchbacks had to be incorporated to cope with the elevation gain, and owing to the terrain, Gold Creek had to be trestled some 25 times. In 1903 the company suffered a major financial setback when the entire southern portion of the rail line had to be rebuilt following its obliteration by the Frank Slide. Another disaster struck in 1910 when a forest fire swept through the valley, destroying all the trestles. Heavy snowfall, too, caused problems. In 1911, the Lille mines were forced to close for a week while the miners were sent to clear snow from the track. These problems, combined with the expense of maintaining the line and the railway equipment, constantly drained the Lille profits. Nevertheless, West Canadian Collieries thought the expense and trouble were worth it—at least until the quality of coal from the Lille mines began to falter. A pass-wide strike in 1911, which lasted eight months, combined with the increasing amount of rock in the coal proved too much for the company. It closed all the Lille mines, the town of Lille and lastly the Frank and Grassy Mountain Railway in 1913. Everything that could be salvaged was skidded out on the cart trail. Then the company tore up the tracks.

*The Frank and Grassy Mountain railbed leading out from Lille.*

# Lille

Originally known as French Camp, Lille was the first of several towns and mines run by a French/Belgium consortium, West Canadian Collieries. Begun by J. J. Fleutot and C. Remy who had been prospecting for gold, Lille mushroomed from a prospecting coal camp in 1901 to a town of more than 400 people with a bakery, a hospital, miners' cottages, rooming houses, a butcher shop, a barber shop, a doctor's office, a school, a general store and a post office—all by 1907. J. J. Fleutot took advantage of his position with the company to erect a substantial hotel, as every town needed a hotel to house visitors and even workers who were waiting for accommodation to become available. When the miners clamoured for a wash house to wash up and change after their shift, the company tried to put off their demands by saying the miners could use the washrooms at the hotel—for a small fee!

The Lille tipple, completed in 1905, was capable of processing 1,000 tonnes of coal per shift. Total coal production at the Lille mines in 1903 was a mere 10,000 tonnes but production rose to 60,000 tonnes the following year. Lille had three operating mines that produced some 900,000 tonnes of bituminous coal in the site's 11 year history. Eventually, the vagaries of the marketplace and increasingly poor quality coal forced the company to make the painful decision to close the mines, and thus the town in 1913. West Canadian Collieries did not cease to exist though. The company already had two profitable mines, Bellevue, which was the first mine the company opened in 1903, and Blairmore South, which began production in 1909. Everything that could be salvaged for the mines at Bellevue and Blairmore was removed from Lille. Mining equipment was transported to Bellevue on the Frank and Grassy Mountain Railway while houses were skidded out on a cart trail paralleling Gold Creek. Today, houses reputedly constructed from lumber from demolished buildings in Lille can be viewed opposite the Mohawk tipple on Highway 3.

*View of Lille townsite, 1907. Photo R. A. Bird.*
*Courtesy Glenbow Archives, ND 10-134.*

# 9 GRASSY MOUNTAIN

Grassy Mountain offers one of the more dramatic tramps in the Crowsnest Pass. From the top of the mountain and its worked seam you are treated to exhilarating views that stretch from the snow-capped peaks of Waterton Lakes National Park in the south to Kananaskis Country in the north.

From the trailhead, retrace your steps to the main mine road and turn left. Follow the road that begins to switchback along the east flank of Grassy Mountain. Finally, at the top of the switchbacks at the base of the worked coal seam bear left and walk up the worked seam through struggling raspberry bushes and wildflowers to a view of the summit that still lies far off in the distance. But the way is clear: across and down the small slack heaps, then up a long grassy slope. In the spring this hillside is a blanket of flowers among which are saskatoon and balsamroot.

Ignore an old road that bisects the hill halfway up and continue scrambling up the slope to the top. Here is another road. Turn left and follow it to the edge of the ridge for a terrific view of the open pit mine workings, backdropped by a glorious view of nearly 360 degrees. Only the Livingstone Range to

**Duration** day

**Distance** 12.2 km

**Level of Difficulty** Moderate elevation gain on open ridge and four-wheel-drive road. Scree descent.

**Maximum Elevation** 2065 m

**Elevation Gain** 488 m

**Map** Blairmore 82 G/9

## Access

From the Blairmore Centre access off Highway 3 drive north on Grassy Mountain road for 9 km to a crossroads at the base of Grassy Mountain. Turn left and park your vehicle.

| | |
|---|---|
| 0 m | trailhead at the base of Grassy Mountain |
| 7.0 km | top of switchbacks |
| 8.0 km | road at the top of the ridge |
| 9.7 km | ruins |
| 10.5 km | bottom of worked seam |
| 12.2 km | trailhead |

Grassy Mountain open pit mine.

*"The Pod" on Grassy Mountain. Courtesy Provincial Museum of Alberta, PG 86.4.5.*

the east blocks views of the plains beyond. Otherwise, your sight line takes in the high, craggy peaks to the south and west as well as Kananaskis Country to the north. From here, the road swings southwest, paralleling the worked seam. This part of the hike affords wonderful views of Crowsnest Mountain, the Seven Sisters and straight ahead, the Flathead Range. Continue on the road across a "bridge" that spans two sections of the seam. Past the "bridge" the road swings around to some dilapidated and flattened buildings on the next ridge. Because all coal was trucked out to West Canadian Collieries' Greenhill tipple at Blairmore, no tipple operations were needed here, explaining the few number of support buildings. There are, though, remains of some storage sheds and a repair shop. Some of the extant buildings are still sitting on their original skids that brought them to this final resting spot. From here, you can look down on the seam as it extends over the next line of mountains below to the West Canadian Collieries' mine at Boisjoli.

The best descent—and the fastest—is straight down through the worked seam. The slack is small and makes the descent quick and invigorating. The bottom of the seam is obvious as trees block the view of the workings and the lakes directly below. Here, turn left and follow the road down the switchback to your vehicle.

Officially named in 1915, Grassy Mountain was a descriptive name given to this 2065 m-high mountain by M. P. Bridgland, a surveyor with the Dominion Land Survey who conducted extensive surveys of the Rocky Mountains. Since then the workings of a post-Second World War open pit coal mine have destroyed the mountain's verdant nature.

## Grassy Mountain Mine

Coal mining in the Crowsnest Pass was a challenge. In the mountain building process, the various layers of rock, including the coal seams, were uplifted and folded, with the result that the coal seams are buckled, twisted and steeply pitched. Where the seams were close to the surface the coal could be removed by open pit mining. Safer than underground mining, open pit mining became the preferred option for coal companies after the Second World War when new technology allowed the vegetation and overburden of dirt and rock to be removed, exposing the coal seams that lay close to the surface.

The Grassy Mountain open pit mine dates from 1947 when West Canadian Collieries undertook open pit mining on the mountain to offset its aging Greenhill and Bellevue mines. To remove the large amount of rock and coal, the mining company employed both trucks and shovels, and draglines, working the seams so that the pit walls rose in a series of terraces. Coal was then removed and trucked down to the tipple at West Canadian Collieries' Greenhill mine site. The magnificent seams were worked until 1957 when market failure forced not only the closure of this open pit mine, but all of the mines owned by West Canadian Collieries.

## No. 2 Coal Seam

Of the four major coal seams that were worked on Grassy Mountain, the most noteworthy is No. 2 seam. It is an excellent example of a seam that, during the mountain building process, was thickened when it was repeatedly folded and faulted. No. 2 seam would normally have been about 6 m thick, but folding and faulting has thickened it to 25 m thick! Known as the "Pod" or the "Big Show," the seam can be viewed on the south face of the mountain, near the top.

*A close-up of "The Pod." Courtesy Provincial Museum of Alberta, PG 86.4.8.*

*Opposite: This coal car is among some of the debris left at the top of Grassy Mountain. Photo Ron Mussieux.*

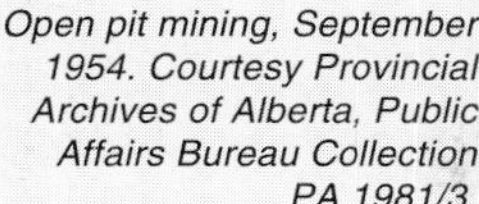

*Open pit mining, September 1954. Courtesy Provincial Archives of Alberta, Public Affairs Bureau Collection PA 1981/3.*

# 10 TWIN LAKES LOOP

As an introduction to the pass and its coal mining history, this is an excellent walk. A now quiet open pit mine at Grassy Mountain with its magnificent worked seam and the ruins of the abandoned surface plant of the Boisjoli underground mine are the highlights of this easy half-day hike.

**Duration** half day
**Distance** 5.2 km return
**Level of Difficulty** Easy walk on four-wheel-drive roads.
**Maximum Elevation** 1555 m
**Elevation Gain** 122 m
**Map** Blairmore 82 G/9

## Access

From the Blairmore Centre access of Highway 3 drive north on Grassy Mountain road for 9 km to a crossroads at the base of Grassy Mountain. Turn left and park your vehicle.

| | |
|---|---|
| 0 m | trailhead at the base of Grassy Mountain |
| 400 m | T-junction |
| 1.7 km | base of worked seam |
| 2.7 km | Boisjoli mine site |
| 5.2 km | Grassy Mountain |

From your vehicle head west along the road on which you parked your vehicle. Be careful, for this road runs along a lip of a steep cliff that plunges to the two lakes below. For a quick look at the open pit mine before heading down to Boisjoli, bear to the right at a T-junction. This road will bring you to the base of the spectacular worked seam that appears to cleave Grassy Mountain in two. A scramble up the worked seam affords an awesome view of the entire seam as it extends south along the ridges to the Boisjoli mine.

Return to the T-junction and continue following the road down to the lakes where the view up the seam is equally impressive. From here, the road loops west and south until it enters the north end of the Boisjoli mine site. Because Boisjoli is located in an open field, there are excellent vistas of the mountains to the west.

Take a few minutes to explore Boisjoli before you circle back to your vehicle. Another of West Canadian Collieries' mine sites, Boisjoli was an underground mine associated with the Greenhill plant. Coal from both Boisjoli and Grassy Mountain were trucked out to the Greenhill surface plant for processing, which is why there were no tipple facilities at either mine. Much of the Boisjoli site has been bulldozed, but the concrete fan house and part of its drift are still situated by the road, and across the road and upslope you can find yet another fan.

Turn left and walk back up to your parked vehicle via the main Grassy Mountain road.

*Grassy Mountain open pit mine as seen from the lakes.*

# 11 COUGAR VALLEY-BOISJOLI LOOP

This hike visits two later West Canadian Collieries' mine sites, Cougar Valley and Boisjoli, which used the tipple facilities of the Greenhill mine when that mine showed signs of petering out. While the main tipple operations remained at Greenhill, the owners built support structures at both of these new mines.

Start your investigation of the Cougar Valley site by walking up the road on the slope to the right. A ventilation fan *sans* its house sits close to the road. Fans were necessary to all the mines. Foul air and methane gas that escaped from the coal face made underground mining dangerous. To reduce the risk of gas explosions, fans, either exhaust (where the foul air was drawn out) or intake (where fresh air was forced into the mine), were installed above the seams. Above the fan you can still find the foundations of an unknown building. Retrace your steps and continue on the road.

At the dam and pool detour to the right onto an old miner's trail. On your left is yet another fan *sans* its house. Return to the main road.

**Duration** half day
**Distance** 6.9 km
**Level of Difficulty** A mix of four-wheel-drive roads, rough trails and bushwhacking.
**Maximum Elevation** 1585 m
**Elevation Gain** 91 m
**Map** Blairmore 82 G/9

## Access

From the Blairmore Centre access off Highway 3 drive north on the Grassy Mountain road for 4.4 km to the far end of a large open clearing, a landfill site that spreads out to both sides of the road. At the end of the clearing, turn right onto a poorly marked road that in less than 1 km brings you to the surface plant of the West Canadian Collieries' Cougar Valley surface facility. Park on the north side of the road.

*Fan at Cougar Valley mine site.*

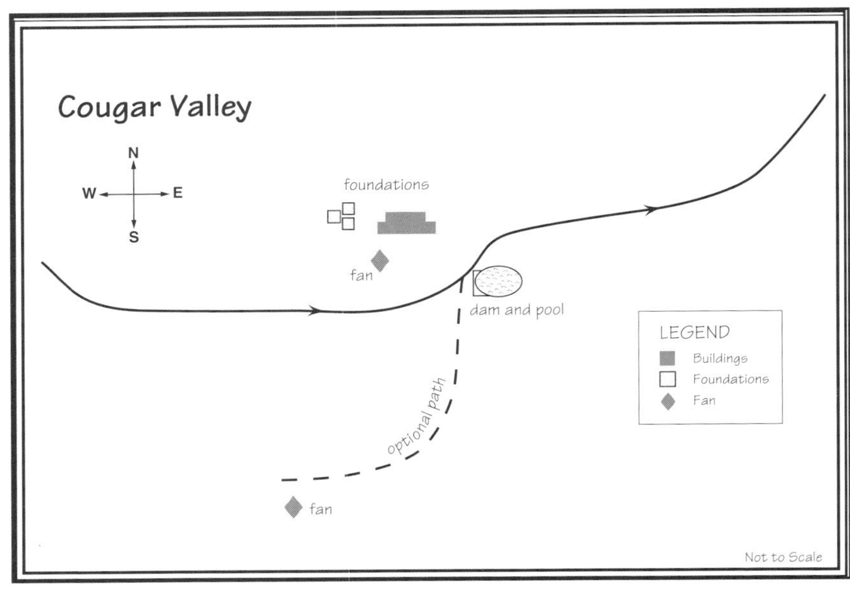

*Fan house and drift, Boisjoli mine.*

## Mining the Coal

There was almost always more than one entry at any mine site. The main entry was the largest, most heavily supported by timbers and was the entry along which the haulage system moved and the air, fresh or foul, flowed. Other entries, called counter entries, cut across the seams more or less at right angles. Because the coal seams in the pass are steeply pitched, the only way to extract the coal was to employ a system called "room and pillar." Miners worked the seam by driving up it in "rooms" 3 m to 5 m wide that were divided roughly in half with a brattice cloth separating the two sections. The coal face constantly seeped lethal methane gas and to disperse the gases the miners used brattice cloth, which was nonporous, to channel the fresh air up one side of the "room," across the coal face and down the other side. Located on the opposite side of the brattice cloth from the coal face was a chute usually lined with metal. The miners shovelled their coal from the face to the chute where, with the help of workers called "buckers," the coal dropped to the entry tunnel. A door at the bottom of the chute could be raised or lowered depending on whether a coal car was available to haul the mined coal to the surface. The "rooms" were separated from each other by 15 m-wide pillars of coal. Every 18 m or so, the miners dug out crosscut tunnels to connect the "rooms."

*Measuring the convergence of strata stress, ca. 1951. Courtesy Provincial Archives of Alberta, Archives Collection A 9902.*

Turn right and follow the road uphill from the surface plant. Part way along, if you wish to explore more remains related to the Cougar Valley site, turn left at the first fork. At one time, a mine entry was located along this roadway. Retrace your steps to the main road and continue uphill to a field below Bluff Mountain on the right. Continue across the field to the far end of the clearing where you can find a pleasant old road that heads north through the forest with occasional views of Grassy Mountain. The road ends at a horse corral. But it is only a short bushwhack through to the Grassy Mountain road, so follow the corral fence toward the slack piles of the Boisjoli mine. Arriving at the main road, turn left and explore the Boisjoli site.

This mine also dates from a much later period than the Greenhill mine, but while many of the post-Second World War mines were open pit, West Canadian Collieries still had to employ underground techniques at both its Cougar Valley and Boisjoli mines. An impressive concrete fan house and a small part of its drift give some indication of the importance of this site.

After exploring Boisjoli, follow the road to Blairmore down the hill to the large, open clearing. This area was once a forested ravine, but in the early 1990s the trees were bulldozed to make way for a large amount of coal slack that was removed from behind the Best Canadian Motor Inn in Blairmore. Turn left and return to the Cougar Valley site and your vehicle.

| | |
|---|---|
| 0 m | trailhead |
| 300 m | fork |
| 900 m | field |
| 3.2 km | horse corral |
| 4.2 km | Boisjoli surface plant |
| 6.2 km | clearing |
| 6.9 km | return to trailhead |

# 12 GREENHILL RIDGE WALK

After visiting the remains of the large surface plant and ancillary off-site buildings of West Canadian Collieries Greenhill mine, this hike takes you to the top of Greenhill Ridge where there are more points of interest and a view of the pass.

**Duration** half day
**Distance** 7.7 km return
**Level of Difficulty** Moderate elevation gain via four-wheel-drive road.
**Maximum Elevation** 1768 m
**Elevation Gain** 427 m
**Map** Blairmore 82 G/9

## Access

Turn north at the Blairmore Centre access off Highway 3 onto the Grassy Mountain road. Located 500 m later on the other side of a cattleguard is the Greenhill surface plant. Park here.

The Greenhill surface plant has a number of buildings still standing that are associated with the operation of any major mine. The first artifact located to the right just past the cattleguard is a small fan. Beyond here, located on the left-hand side of the road, are a store- and electrical house, and a small dynamite shed. The use of dynamite in mines known to seep dangerous gases is an interesting story. Because most miners were contract workers, they were paid by the amount of coal they dug. It was in their interest, then, to free as much coal as possible. First, using only a pick, the miners dug either a horizontal or a vertical

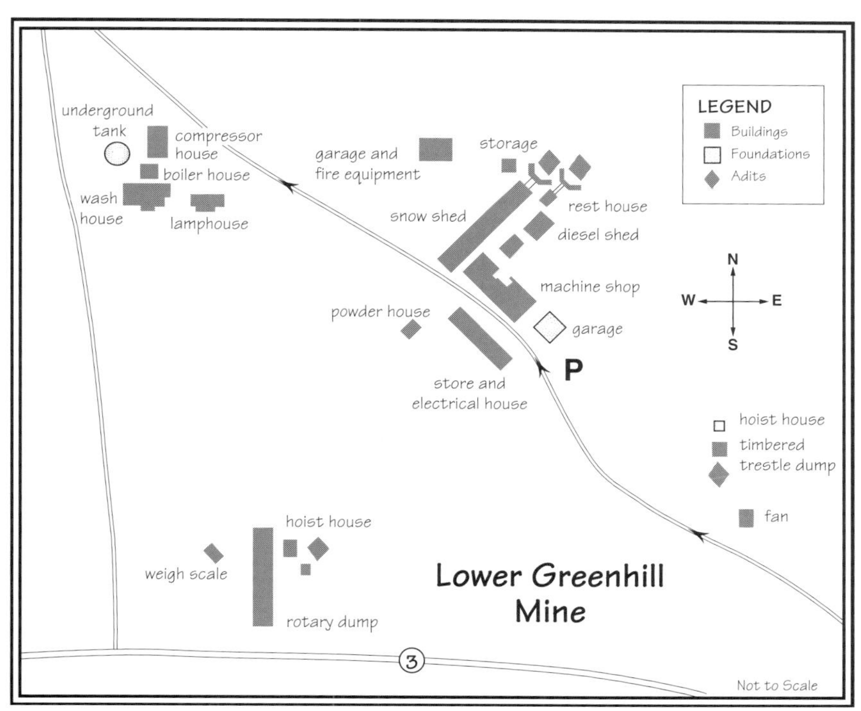

Mine opening as seen from the snowshed at the lower Greenhill mine site.

trench in the coal face. This provided space into which the coal could expand when the charge was lit. However, digging trenches was slow work and many miners preferred to use dynamite to shoot from a solid face without first digging a trench. Having no room into which it could expand, the explosion often shot back into the room, maiming or even killing the miners. Owners tried to resist the extensive use of dynamite because it produced too much slack coal, the small pieces that were only usable for coking. In 1916, when West Canadian Collieries tried to reduce the number of sticks of dynamite from three to two for each miner on shift, the miners walked off their jobs.

Take a moment to walk behind the dynamite shed to the remains of a weigh scale partially surrounded by a rusting barbed-wire fence. Do not cross the barbed wire; the wooden loading platform has rotted and you will have a nasty fall. To the left of the weigh scale is the rotary dump. Here, coal was dumped into the tipple to be cleaned and sorted prior to being loaded into railway cars. The loaded coal cars from the mine entered the dump and hooked onto a mechanism that turned the car 180 degrees and upside down. The coal dropped into the tipple proper below. A

**Note**: Greenhill is a designated Provincial Historic Site and may not be disturbed.

| | |
|---|---|
| 0 m | Greenhill mine surface plant |
| 400 m | fork |
| 800 m | hoist house |
| 1.5 km | fan house |
| 3.5 km | ridge top |
| 5.2 km | fork and fan house |
| 6.1 km | mine site |
| 7.7 km | return to trailhead |

rotary dump, complete with a coal car, is still inside the remains of the tipple structure. However, now the site has been secured with a chain link fence owing to the dangerous condition of the structure.

Back at the road on the opposite side from the dynamite shed is a long snow shed that protected the rail track all the way back to the mine opening that now has been dynamited closed. Farther along the road are other buildings. The first one you reach is the lamphouse on the left side of the road. In the early days miners had open flame lamps attached to their caps, a dangerous procedure because of the increased likelihood of a dust or gas explosion. But when safety lamps were introduced around 1910, the miners protested. The safety lamps' "dim and uncertain light" was deemed to be more dangerous than the open flame lamp. But safety concerns prevailed. The lamps were kept in the lamphouse where a lamp man cleaned and examined each lamp before issuing it to a miner. Later, safety lamps were replaced by electric headlights that received their power from a battery pack carried on the miner's hip.

The wash house located at the bend in the road and now boarded up was the change room for the miners before and after their shift. It had lockers along the walls and down the centre aisle. Wash houses were a contentious issue between the miners and the owners in the early days. Owners did not wish to erect such expensive ancillary buildings, whereas miners demanded a place to wash off the coal dust and change into clean clothes. West Canadian Collieries, initially reluctant to build wash houses at any of its mines, was forced to build these structures. The boiler and compressor houses, located next to the wash house, were crucial support for the underground operation.

After exploring this lower site, walk farther along the Grassy Mountain road, then branch right at a fork. Four hundred metres along the mine road keep left at a junction. Just beyond is

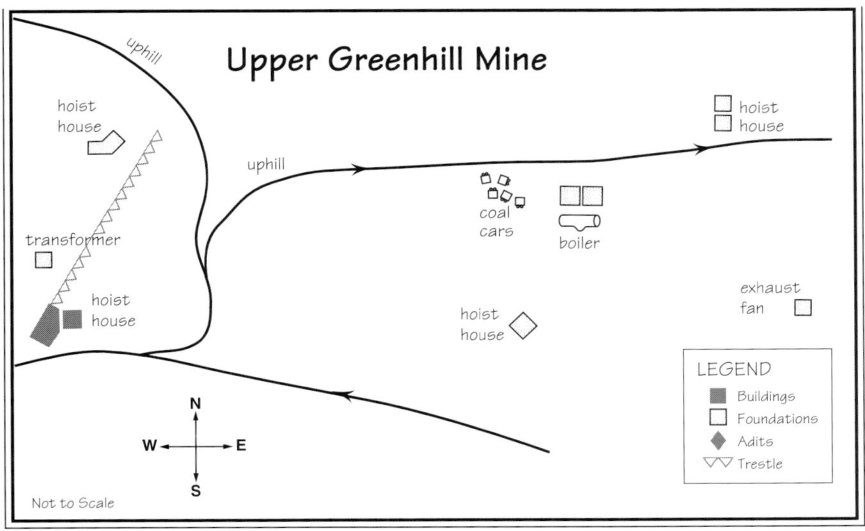

## Rock Fall!

Mine roofs collapsing and other rock falls were always a danger in the underground mines in the Crowsnest Pass. In February 1930, Frank Bombadier and his partner, Frank Cizek, were preparing to mine the coal at their workplace when, without any warning, a rock fall pinned them down. Fortunately, the rock fall occurred about the time that the fireboss, who always conducted a safety check prior to blasting, was due at the mens' workplace. Rescue crews began work almost immediately but it was many long hours before the crews located the two miners and by then Cizek was dead.

## The Greenhill Mine

For 44 years, the ridge that extends north of Highway 3 at Blairmore was the scene of perhaps the most successful mine in the pass. The Greenhill mine, opened in 1913 by West Canadian Collieries at a time when it was forced to close operations at Lille and at Blairmore South, remained one of the company's most profitable mines until failing markets forced the mine's closure in 1957. Its 500 to 600 men produced some 3,000 tonnes a day during the 1940s, with the best year being 1946 when production went over the top with 758,000 tonnes. Production dropped after the Second World War as railways switched from coal to diesel. The company, though, tried to wait out the recession and it was only in 1962 that West Canadian Collieries admitted defeat and went out of business. Throughout its long career the Greenhill mine and its adjacent mines at Cougar Valley and Boisjoli produced a noteworthy 14,000,000 tonnes of coal!

*Rotary dump. Courtesy Provincial Archives of Alberta, Archives Collection A 6154.*

*Fan at upper Greenhill mine site.*

an old hoist house complete with its machinery. Scramble up the slope behind to an old road above. Follow it to the right, disregarding all spurs. You will come to some coal cars and a boiler on the right side of the road. Continue along the roadway to a fan.

To gain the top of Greenhill Ridge, follow the four-wheel-drive track from the fan uphill. A line of subsidence pits parallels the track all the way up to the top. If you wish to examine any of them, be very careful. Halfway along, the track is strewn with the ruins of hollow red brick buildings and stockpiled rough-sawn timbers. The red hollow bricks were West Canadian Collieries' "trademark" building material and you will find that most of its buildings associated with either the Bellevue or Greenhill mines were built of this brick.

Beyond here, the track braids. The lower braid to the right offers protection from prevailing west winds that often blow strongly through the pass. The summit affords fine views of the entire length of the pass as well as of Grassy Mountain and its old open pit mine to the north and Crowsnest Mountain and the Seven Sisters to the west.

To return, double back to the meadow, keeping alert for subsidence. Descend the ridge by taking a path that starts from behind the site of a former fan. Cross under power lines and at a fork bear right onto a road that leads to No. 3 level mine entry, the upper mine site of the Greenhill mine complex. Here there is a mine opening and a large fan that can still be found perched at the edge of the hill.

Continue along the road to the hoist house and from there to the Greenhill surface plant and your vehicle.

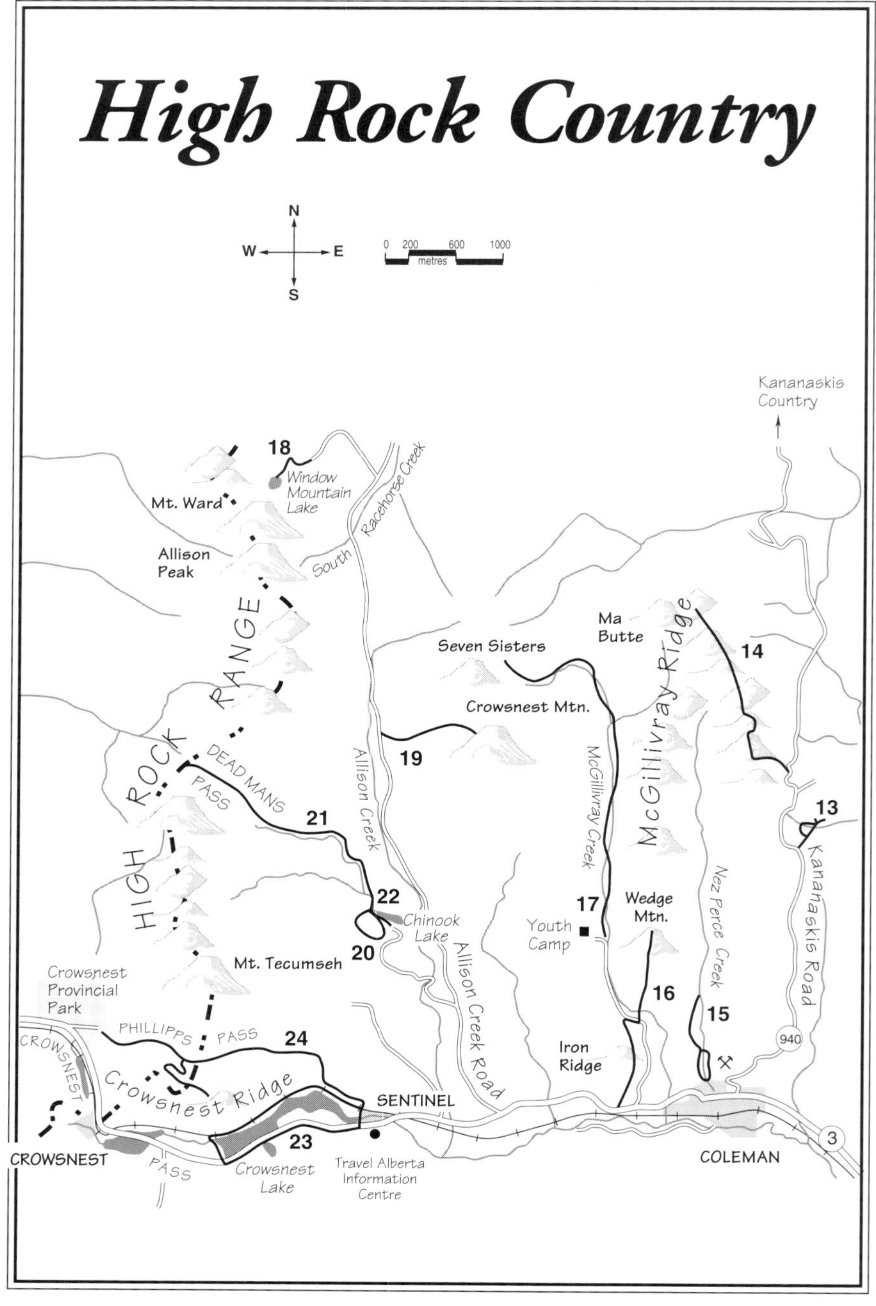

High Rock Country
N
W
E
S
0 200 600 1000
metres
Kananaskis Country
18
Window Mountain Lake
Mt. Ward
South Racehorse Creek
Allison Peak
HIGH ROCK RANGE
Ma Butte
McGillivray Ridge
14
Seven Sisters
Crowsnest Mtn.
19
DEAD MANS PASS
Allison Creek
McGillivray Creek
21
13
Kananaskis Road
Nez Perce Creek
22
17
Wedge Mtn.
Chinook Lake
Youth Camp
20
Allison Creek Road
Mt. Tecumseh
Crowsnest Provincial Park
16
15
PHILLIPPS PASS
24
940
Iron Ridge
CROWSNEST
Crowsnest Ridge
SENTINEL
23
3
CROWSNEST
PASS
Crowsnest Lake
Travel Alberta Information Centre
COLEMAN

# Coleman

A. C. Flumerfelt, the president of International Coal and Coke Company, oversaw the development of the townsite located adjacent to his mine in 1903. Once the town lots had been surveyed, he named the settlement Coleman after his youngest daughter, Florence Coleman Flumerfelt.

Sprawling on both sides of Highway 3 west of Blairmore is the town of Coleman. As you drive by the strip of motels and eateries you have little hint that this community was one of the most economically vibrant coal mining towns in the pass.

Three brothers from Spokane, Frank, William and Jay Graves, had invested in the development of low grade copper deposits in southern British Columbia. To smelt the copper they needed a cheap supply of both coal and coke. Knowledge of the bituminous coal fields of the Crowsnest Pass prompted them to purchase properties here in 1903 and to hire A. C. Flumerfelt, a businessman from Victoria, B.C., with a solid track record in finance and industry, as the first president of the newly formed International Coal and Coke Company. By the autumn, a townsite had been surveyed and within a year businessmen had moved into the new mining community. Once the mine was in production, the company built the first 74 coke ovens, later building more to bring the total to 216. Some of the ovens, rebuilt in 1932, can be viewed from the south end of 75 Street in downtown Coleman.

Another coal company, McGillivray Creek Coal and Coke Company, began mining the seams north of the Canadian Pacific Railway in 1909. With two large mines in town, Coleman grew dramatically. Today, a drive along 17 and 18 avenues between 79 and 75 streets will give you an idea of the businesses, benevolent societies, mine offices, churches and residences that graced the Coleman's core. Many residences were built south of the railway tracks where you can still see many miners' cottages en route to some of the trailheads.

In 1910, self assurance prompted Coleman to incorporate a settlement known as Slav Town located west of the main townsite. Known for its east European population, Slav Town was strictly a residential area where the miners lived in cottages laid out in neat rows. If you wish to visit Slav Town, now long known as West Coleman, drive west along 18 Avenue.

*Coleman coke ovens, ca. 1912. Courtesy Glenbow Archives, NA 2004-1.*

*The coke ovens today.*

# 13 PELLETIER LUMBER CAMP

In late summer this modest hike proves a boon to those of you who like gathering wild mushrooms. Orange capped boletus is just one of the numerous edible species found scattered about the forest floor. Along the way is evidence of a Pelletier lumber camp.

Begin at the cutline. Right at the trailhead, turn left at a fork onto an old road. At a second fork, bear right; this leads back to the cutline. Keep a sharp eye out and a short distance along the cutline turn left once again to rejoin the old road that meanders into the woods. Throughout this area is evidence of man's presence. The road degenerates into a path, swings to the left and descends a small ridge at the bottom of which are the remains of an old bridge associated with a Pelletier sawmill camp.

Cross the stream and skirt it. Located slightly up the hill are notched timbers and a large iron pulley lying at the edge of a gully. Follow a path to the right that leads to a recrossing of the stream and hence back to the cutline. Turn left and after crossing the stream, walk up the steep cutline. At the top of the rise turn left on an old road leading to the remains of a log bunkhouse with saddle notched corners. Sawmill camps were established as homes away from home for the men who cut and skidded the felled timbers out to the mills.

Return the way you came as far as the curve in the old road. Here a path leads off to the right up over the ridge. Fifty metres later at a fork bear left. Farther along this pleasant old logging road another left fork returns you to the edge of the sawmill camp. Cross the stream, turn left and follow the path out to the cutline.

If you wish to view the remains of a flume system cross the stream and climb the cutline ridge to the right of the aforementioned route to the bunkhouse. Situated three-quarters of the way up the ridge is a path heading off to the right. Go left at a fork; a short distance beyond is the flume. Retrace you steps to the cutline. Turn left to return to your vehicle.

**Duration** 1 hour
**Distance** 2.6 km return
**Level of Difficulty** Easy walk on woodland paths.
**Maximum Elevation** 1738 m
**Elevation Gain** negligible
**Map** Blairmore 82 G/9

## Access

From Coleman drive 7.9 km north on SR 940 (Kananaskis Road) that leads to Kananaskis Country. At a Nova gas pipeline cut, pull off to the right and park.

| | |
|---|---|
| 0 m | trailhead |
| 80 m | second fork |
| 300 m | old road |
| 400 m | saw camp |
| 500 m | stream |
| 800 m | old road |
| 1.1 km | bunkhouse |
| 1.4 km | path |
| 1.7 km | fork and saw camp |
| 1.9 km | path |
| 2.0 km | remains of flume |
| 2.6 km | return to trailhead |

## Pelletier Lumber Company

The demand for railway ties and timber for railway bridges at the time of the construction of the Crowsnest Pass line of the Canadian Pacific Railway in 1897-98 gave birth to the first exploitation of the area's natural resources. With the boom in coal mining that followed the construction of the rail line, timbers were needed by the mining companies. Not only was lumber needed for the surface plant buildings, but rough timbers were used extensively underground to shore up the fragile roof over main entries and tunnels. Logging became an important secondary industry. The Pelletier logging concern, begun in 1905 with the erection of a sawmill near the head of Blairmore Creek, operated until sometime in the 1920s, when H. W. Pelletier turned his energies to real estate. Scattered remains are all that are left of this small but vital company.

*Logging crew, ca. 1910. Courtesy Provincial Archives of Alberta, Harry Pollard Collection P 1039.*

## Mushrooms–Orange-capped Boletus

**Scientific Name** *Leccinum aurantiacum*
**Other Name** Red Cap Boletus

Mushrooms are fungi. Fungi have no chlorophyll so they have to obtain their food from other plants or animals, living or dead. Bolete fungi have a symbiotic partnership with tree roots; the fungi provide water and minerals for the tree and the tree roots supply nutrients essential for the growth and development of the mushroom.

Mushroom collecting can be fun with tasty results. But there are many deadly varieties, so if you wish to experiment with any that you collect on this hike, it is only safe to do so after your specimens have been examined and pronounced edible by either an experienced amateur collector or a scientist.

# 14 MCGILLIVRAY RIDGE

**Duration** half day
**Distance** 6.4 km return
**Level of Difficulty** Steep climb. Bushwhacking and hard-packed road.
**Maximum Elevation** 2359 m
**Elevation Gain** 591 m
**Map** Crowsnest 82 G/10

## Access

Drive 10.4 km north from Coleman on SR 940 (Kananaskis Road) that leads to Kananaskis Country. At a curve in the road find an old grassy roadbed on the left. Park here.

| | |
|---|---|
| 0 m | trailhead |
| 160 m | T-junction |
| 500 m | double hydro poles |
| 1.4 km | TransAlta road |
| 2.9 km | telecommunication station |
| 3.2 km | cairn on top of McGillivray Ridge |
| 6.4 km | return to trailhead |

This was the ridge that the McGillivray Coal & Coke Company of Coleman mined for bituminous coal, although you will see no evidence of mining activity along this hike.

While short, this hike offers significant elevation gain over a short distance to a telecommunication station en route to the highest point of McGillivray Ridge.

Walk up the grassy road for approximately 160 m to a T-junction with a hydro cutline. Turn right to climb to the double hydro poles. Here, the hydro line and your route take a 90 degree turn uphill. Cutlines are avoided as hiking trails in most circumstances. But do not let the steep climb through salmonberries, strawberries and small alders discourage you from what is otherwise a terrific hike. From the top of the last steep pull it is but a short distance to a TransAlta four-wheel-drive road. Turn right.

The steepness of the first part of the hike relents only a little as the road winds up grassy McGillivray Ridge. At the top of the shoulder the road finally flattens out and winds around a horseshoe turn toward a telecommunications station. Nip over to the station for spectacular views of the eastern slopes of Crowsnest Mountain and the Seven Sisters. To the east the white limestone of the Livingstone Range stretches a long way north beyond the open pit mine on Grassy Mountain and the green slopes of Bluff Mountain.

Return to the horse–shoe bend and strike across scree and grass, later using an old road to aid you in the steep pull up to the highest part of this ridge system. A climb along the spine to the summit brings Ma Butte and Crowsnest Mountain into view again as well as a total 360 degree panorama. Look across to the east

*TransAlta telecommunications tower with summit spine of McGillivray Ridge to right. Photo Gillean Daffern.*

*Looking across McGillivray Creek to the eastern slopes of Crowsnest Mountain and the Seven Sisters. Photo Gillean Daffern.*

face of Ma Butte. You will notice the various rock strata lie in flat layers. Ma Butte and McGillivray Ridge are part of the same geological formation called the Blairmore Group, and as such are unfaulted, a rare phenomena in the pass. Ma Butte also marks the northerly limit of the Crowsnest volcanics (see Wedge Mountain trail).

Walk back south down the ridge and before returning to the road, add a rock to the cairn overlooking the telecommunications station.

## McGillivray Ridge

There are two possible origins to the name of this ridge. The first relates to William McGillivray (b.1764 - d.1825) of the 18th and 19th centuries' fur trading concern the North West Company, of which he was chief director. Drawn into the fur trade by his uncle Simon McTavish, McGillivray served as a wintering partner for several seasons before becoming superintendent of the northwest trade. He was made chief director of the company in 1804 upon the death of McTavish. For the next 17 years he led the company through a period of intense rivalry with the Hudson's Bay Company. This ended in 1821 with the amalgamation of the two companies under the name of the Hudson's Bay Company. He became a director of the new company until his death in 1825. McGillivray was an energetic man who also served in the House of Assembly of Lower Canada (now Quebec) in 1808 and again from 1814 to 1825. During the War of 1812 he lead a company of voyageurs in General Brock's successful attack on Detroit.

The other possible origin of the name McGillivray Ridge relates to the coal mining company, McGillivray Creek Coal & Coke Company of Coleman, that mined this ridge for its bituminous coal. The McGillivray Creek Coal & Coke Company operated from 1909 to the mid-1930s when it and International Coal & Coke of Coleman were taken over by Consolidated Mining and Smelting Company Limited.

# 15 OLD MINER'S PATH

The trail up Nez Perce Creek makes a pleasant evening stroll after a full day of hiking elsewhere in the pass. It is also where you can meet many of the local residents taking the evening air. This trail follows a path once used by the miners of McGillivray Creek Coal & Coke Company to get to their surface plant. This historic path has been upgraded by the Coleman Lion's Club as far as a waterfall. The remainder of the hike is along ungroomed but obvious paths.

**Duration** 1 hour
**Distance** 4.6 km return
**Level of Difficulty** Easy walk on groomed and social paths.
**Maximum Elevation** 1463 m
**Elevation Gain** 122 m
**Map** Crowsnest 82 G/10

## Access

From Highway 3 at the west end of Coleman turn onto 76 St. Almost immediately there is a fork. Take the right-hand fork and descend to Flumerfelt Park. Park at the Coleman Information Centre (kiosk) and follow the Miner's Path signs.

The groomed path leads north, winding through the pleasant valley of Nez Perce Creek. Cross a bridge and continue to a second bridge and a set of stairs. Ignore the stairs and continue along the path that now enters a ravine with moss-lined walls offering a cool respite after a warm day. A second bridge over the creek is to be ignored as well. Continue on the east side of the creek along the path, passing through a white gate to a small waterfall that indicates the end of the formal trail. Scramble up the east bank to follow another path continuing north to an old dam site and a modern concrete flume. Cross Nez Perce Creek to the west

*The Old Miner's Path along Nez Perce Creek.*

| | |
|---|---|
| 0 m | trailhead at the Coleman Information Centre (kiosk) |
| 700 m | waterfall |
| 900 m | dam and concrete flume |
| 1.4 km | end of the road |
| 3.2 km | return to dam |
| 4.2 km | McGillivray mine yard and fork |
| 4.6 km | return to the trailhead |

*Nez Perce Creek.*

## Nez Perce Creek

Translated, Nez Perce means "pierced nose." It was the name given by the French to a group of Indian tribes in the United States who pierced their noses so they could adorn themselves with shells. Today, Nez Perce refers to a specific tribe found in northern Idaho and Oregon. How did the name of an American Indian tribe come to be used for a creek north of the border?

The story begins in Montana in 1877 when the Nez Perce under Chief Joseph were forced by the American government to leave Montana and move to Idaho. Along the way, a young Nez Perce warrior killed four settlers to avenge their murder of his father. The U.S. Cavalry gave chase, one that resulted in 18 skirmishes between the soldiers and the Nez Perce, four of them outright battles. The Nez Perce were on the run. They were hoping to find refuge in Canada much as the Sioux had the previous year after the Battle of the Little Big Horn. More than 2700 km later the Nez Perce made their last stand only 48 km south of the border. Rather than see his people slaughtered, Chief Joseph negotiated peace with the Americans. However, some 150-200 of his people did escape across the border. They were given sanctuary at Fort Walsh in the Cypress Hills where the escaped Sioux had congregated. Later, the Nez Perce resettled in the Pincher Creek and Fort Macleod areas and some moved onto the Peigan Reserve at Brocket.

## The McGillivray Creek Coal & Coke Company

Coal seams in the Crowsnest Pass increase in thickness and number as you move west and south. For example, at Blairmore there are three major seams, but at Coleman there are five seams running perpendicular to both the pass and the railway line, thereby allowing maximum accessibility. The bituminous seams under the town of Coleman were tapped by two competing companies, the International Coal and Coke Company beginning in 1903 and in 1909 by the McGillivray Creek Coal & Coke Company, which worked the seams north of the Canadian Pacific Railway line. In its first year of operation, McGillivray extracted a mere 150 tonnes a day. But once the tipple and a ventilation system were built, daily production figures jumped to 50,000 tonnes in 1910.

In the early years there were enough customers to allow close competition between International Coal and Coke and McGillivray Creek Coal & Coke Company. However, by the mid-1930s, the economic depression and the increased use of diesel by the railways, the traditional customer of the Crowsnest Pass mines, forced the takeover of both companies by Consolidated Mining and Smelting Company Limited. Consolidated went through an amalgamation with Hillcrest Mohawk at the east end of the pass in 1952, resulting in Coleman Collieries. Coleman Collieries was the last operational mine on Alberta's side of the Crowsnest Pass until it was forced to shut down in 1983.

## Ten Miners Killed

Mining Crowsnest coal was neither an easy nor a risk-free occupation. Many miners were injured, maimed or killed as a result of their job. One of the biggest threats that hung over all the pass mines was the possibility of an explosion. Deadly methane gas trapped in pockets in the coal seams seeped from the coal face. If the gas was not dispersed by a flow of fresh air, a spark from dynamite or from a rock fall or from a careless cigarette could trigger a massive explosion. As miners and mine owners were fond of saying, a mine was only as safe as the stupidest person in it.

What happened at the McGillivray mine on November 23, 1926, will never be known for certain. But the explosion that rocked the mine left three men dead and seven missing. The hero of the hour was Frank Serak who led to safety six men by taking an old crosscut between No. 3 and No. 2 levels where they met with another group of miners who had also narrowly escaped death. From there, Serak followed the signs and messages that Hugh Dunlop, the fireboss, had left for any survivors. Aftershocks hampered rescue attempts. A few days later another body was recovered. To prevent the possible spread of fire, water was pumped into part of the mine. It was only after several months when the company had pumped out the water that the badly decomposed bodies of the six remaining miners were found. Evidence at the inquiry following the disaster suggested the type of explosive used in the mine might have been responsible for igniting the methane gas and dust that were present.

bank where another scramble up the hill leads to an old road. If you wish, follow the road north along the ridge until it disintegrates into a game trail.

Return to the dam. This time, follow a well-marked path leading south along the west bank to the remains of the McGillivray mine yard. At a fork, keep to the right. Before exiting at 74 Street, tarry awhile in the mine yard of one of the pass' major mines. Foundations of various buildings and wooden debris can be found throughout the site. Pass through a gate in the fence at the end of the roadway. From here, the road leads out to 74 Street. A short walk via 24 Avenue (go left) and 76 Street as far as a set of concrete steps that lead down into the park, returns you to your vehicle.

*George Rudeychuk, ca. 1920. Courtesy Provincial Archives of Alberta, Archives Collection A 2419.*

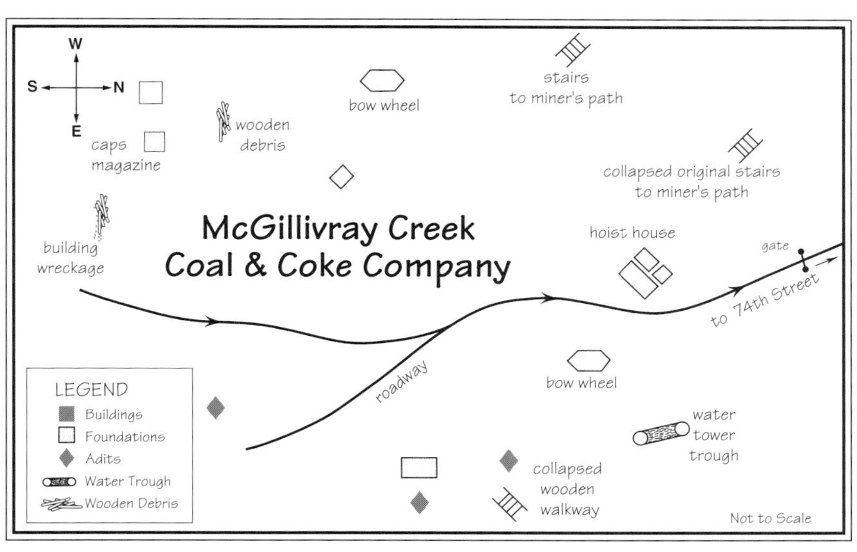

# 16 WEDGE MOUNTAIN TRAIL

Iron Ridge and Wedge Mountain may not be paved in gold, but gold and its legends are very much part of this area's history. No fortunes can be made from this hike, but the views from the ridge and from Wedge Mountain make your effort worthwhile. The tramp up Wedge Mountain is more demanding than it would first appear.

**Duration** half day

**Distance** 8.6 km return

**Level of Difficulty** Open ridge walk with steep sections and scree.

**Maximum Elevation** 1870 m

**Elevation Gain** 762 m

**Map** Crowsnest 82 G/10

From the highway you must gain access to the top of Iron Ridge. Initially it is a scramble up rough scree, but once on the ridge it is a pleasant stroll northward toward Wedge Mountain. Three fences leading to a double set of power lines are your reference points before reaching the end of the furthermost promontory. From here, the south ridge of Wedge Mountain and the trail climbing up it are clearly visible.

## Access

Park at the big Crowsnest Pass sign on the south side of Highway 3 just west of Coleman. Iron Ridge lies across the highway.

| | |
|---|---|
| 0 m | trailhead |
| 700 m | double set of power lines |
| 2.1 km | furthermost promontory on Iron Ridge |
| 2.8 km | base of Wedge Mtn. |
| 4.3 km | top of Wedge Mtn. |
| 8.6 km | return to trailhead |

*An exciting view of Crowsnest Mountain and the Seven Sisters from Wedge Mountain.*

## Wedge Mountain

The name of Wedge Mountain is descriptive of the mountain's shape. While not obvious while walking along Iron Ridge, the wedge-like shape of the mountain can best be seen from Highway 3 west of your trailhead.

## Crowsnest Volcanics

One hundred million years ago during the mountain-building process, there was an explosive volcanic eruption that shot large rocks and ash into the air. Today, evidence of this violent event can be found in a band of volcanic rock extending from Ma Butte in the north to Willoughby Ridge in the south. The Crowsnest Volcanics are among the few known volcanic rocks in Alberta.

The Crowsnest Volcanics are thickest just north of Coleman. This may indicate the location of the ancient volcano that spewed the rock and ash although no evidence of the vent can be spotted on the ground today.

The best place to view the Crowsnest Volcanics is where Highway 3 cuts through Iron Ridge just west of Coleman. It is here, too, that rock hounds can search for black garnets and pink sanidine crystals that have been eroded from the face of the cut and are found at the base of the rock.

*The Crowsnest Volcanics exposed at the road cut on Highway 3 west of Coleman. Photo Ron Mussieux.*

## Gold!

One of the most precious metals, gold has triggered stampedes across mountains and deserts to California and over dangerous passes into the wilds of the Yukon by men and women searching for a new life full of unknowns, dangers, and, if lucky, fortune. It has caused heartbreak more often than elation, and even death. Over its history, the Crowsnest Pass has witnessed some of the hysteria that followed in the wake of discovery.

The first report of gold in the pass or in the country to the north is wrapped in the mists of the 19th century. Reputedly, about 1870, two prospectors, Frank Lemon and "Blackjack," both from Montana, were searching for gold with others north of the 49th parallel. Unsuccessful in their search for gold, they decided to return to Montana. They split off from the main party and joined a party of Indians who were travelling south along the foothills. Then, taking leave of their native companions, the two continued on, searching for gold along the way. At the headwaters of a creek, they made their discovery. By all accounts it was a rich find. But that same night the two men quarrelled terribly and Lemon killed "Blackjack." Grabbing the gold they had found, Lemon returned to Montana. Meanwhile, two Stoney Indians who may or may not have witnessed the actual murder reported the murder to their chief who swore them to silence about the location of the gold.

That might have been the end of the story, but Lemon apparently told of his findings upon his return to Montana. However, he quickly became mentally unstable, possibly owing to a bad conscience. Nevertheless, a number of Montana prospectors persuaded Lemon to lead them to the gold-bearing creek. To the disappointment and fury of the prospectors, Lemon could not locate the creek. Over the years the legend of the "Lost Lemon Mine" has enticed many would-be prospectors into looking for the mother lode, all in vain.

All legends have some basis in fact. Whether the Lemon story has any factual merit or not, it is a fact that gold has been found in the rocks known as the Crowsnest Volcanics. Although outcrops of the volcanics can be seen throughout the pass, they are thickest just east of Crowsnest Mountain along Iron Ridge, Wedge Mountain and north to Ma Butte. In 1989, two Albertans announced their find of gold in the volcanics, and the rush for permits to stake the deposits was on. In the course of that summer, application for permits covering some 29,000 ha were submitted. The hype was short lived. The grade of gold ore was too low to make mining feasible, and the last gold rush in the Crowsnest Pass joined the Lost Lemon Mine in history.

To reach Wedge Mountain, descend Iron Ridge by bushwhacking down the slope to the left to avoid cliffs to the right and straight ahead. Near the bottom a rough road leads down to an intersection with the McGillivray Youth Camp access road. Continue straight ahead, cross the McGillivray access road and follow the track down the slope to the base of Wedge Mountain.

You begin what is a tough pull up to the summit. After an initial bushwhack, most of the elevation gain is made in short but steep spurts through scree. Choose any of the crisscrossing paths. Once into the pine trees and off the loose scree you still have a steady climb to the top where a magnificent panorama awaits you. To the west, Crowsnest Mountain and Seven Sisters are silhouetted against the sky. To the north and east are McGillivray Ridge and the scarred remnants of the modern-day Vicary open pit mine.

Return the way you came.

# 17 TRAIL TO THE SEVEN SISTERS

This hike is your only opportunity to witness up close the majestic eastern slopes of the Seven Sisters. And for those of you who like to poke about old ruins, this hike passes through two old logging camps complete with log bunkhouses and other remains.

From the trailhead return to the fork. Here, bear left and follow McGillivray Creek upstream. The road, which in places is nearly impassable for even four-wheel-drive vehicles, crosses McGillivray Creek several times en route to the Seven Sisters.

At a fork, bear to the right. The road continues through a mixed forest of pine and poplar and crosses two small tributaries. There is yet a third stream crossing. This one is McGillivray Creek and is quite wide, but is liberally strewn with stepping stones. A short distance beyond the crossing the road enters a wide, open field typical

**Duration** day

**Distance** 16 km return

**Level of Difficulty** Gradual elevation gain on hard-packed road and trail.

**Maximum Elevation** 2165 m

**Elevation Gain** 640 m

**Map** Crowsnest 82 G/10

## Access

From Highway 3 at the west end of Coleman turn north onto 61 St. Continue only a short distance to 22 Ave., then turn right. The road forks almost immediately. Take the left-hand fork, 23 Ave., as it climbs out of town. At forks in the road at 3.3 and 3.8 km bear right and pass through the gap between Iron Ridge and Wedge

### *Seven Sisters*

**Previous Name**

The Steeples

It was Lieutenant Thomas Blakiston, magnetical observer attached to the Palliser Expedition (1857-1860), who gave the descriptive name "Steeples" to this 2591 m-high mountain north of Crowsnest Mountain.

Those who settled in the Crowsnest Pass at the turn of the 20th century were unaware of this name and Seven Sisters became a more popular name with the local people. In 1978 the name "Seven Sisters" was adopted officially.

*The Seven Sisters from near the end of the trail.*

of logging camps where crews cleared a sizable area for their home away from home. This camp was almost assuredly one of the McLaren Lumber Company's, dating from the first two decades of the 20th century. The company initially supplied railway ties to the Canadian Pacific Railway and later timbers to the mining companies in the pass. The remnants of a log bunkhouse and scattered evidence of man's occupation of this site are backdropped by the towering silhouettes of Crowsnest Mountain on the left and Ma Butte straight ahead.

Continue along the road to a fork. Keep right. Here the road degenerates quickly into a low swamp beyond which the road is reduced to a mere path resembling a game trail. At the next fork swing right again. The old roadbed reappears at the point where cellar depressions indicate another habitation. The loggers found this part of the country to be low and wet as evidenced by sections of old corduroy still to be found embedded in the roadbed. In another swampy area continue straight ahead at a crossroads. Soon after crossing McGillivray Creek the road begins to climb more perceptibly. Another stream crossing and you break out of the trees into an open field, the site of a second sawmill camp with several cellar depressions, cable and pieces of iron located to the right just beyond the last stream crossing. Ma Butte extends along the entire eastern flank.

At a fork, turn left on a road that now swings sharply to the west and climbs between two hills. Underground springs create more marshy wet spots, some of which can be circumvented by taking paths up the right-hand bank.

Just past this last wet area the road becomes a mere path and leaving McGillivray Creek climbs to the top of a ridge where you get your first good view of the Seven Sisters. It is now but a short descent to a clearing where the path continues to the right, following the small stream almost to the base of the Seven Sisters. The scenery is awe-inspiring; the cliffs and talus slopes are softened somewhat by the wide alpine meadows near its base. To the left, Crowsnest Mountain dominates the skyline.

Return the way you came.

Mountain. Finally, a full km later (4.8 km from Highway 3), there is yet another fork. Turn left and drive up a well-gravelled road to the parking lot at the McGillivray Creek Youth Camp.

| | |
|---|---|
| 0 m | trailhead |
| 200 m | four-wheel-drive road |
| 700 m | series of stream crossings |
| 1.4 km | fork |
| 2.8 km | small stream crossing |
| 3.2 km | second stream crossing |
| 3.5 km | third stream crossing |
| 3.7 km | saw camp |
| 3.9 km | fork |
| 4.1 km | fork |
| 4.5 km | crossroads |
| 4.8 km | stream crossing |
| 5.3 km | stream crossing and saw camp |
| 5.4 km | fork |
| 6.7 km | top of ridge |
| 6.8 km | clearing |
| 8.0 km | slopes of Seven Sisters |
| 16.0 km | return to trailhead |

# 18 WINDOW MOUNTAIN LAKE

What begins as a pleasant but ordinary hike through spruce forest changes dramatically at Window Mountain Lake where you explode with excitement at the wow! sight of a high alpine lake surrounded on three sides by towering cliffs and mountains. Picnic sites and easy trails around the lake make this a favourite with many hikers in the Crowsnest Pass.

From the trailhead the road soon dwindles to a broad path as it begins climbing past strawberry and raspberry patches. Today, instead of heavy forest, young pine and spruce trees compete for your attention with slashes of fireweed, Indian

**Duration** half day
**Distance** 3.8 km return
**Level of Difficulty** Moderate hike on trail.
**Maximum Elevation** 1982 m
**Elevation Gain** 213 m
**Maps** Crowsnest 82 G/10 Tornado Mountain 82 G/15

## Access

From Highway 3 drive north on the Allison Creek road. At a fork in the road 2.7 km later keep right and climb over a low pass into South Racehorse Creek drainage. Approximately 16.8 km from Highway 3 there is a logged area at the bottom of a long hill. At the north end of this old logged area, now partially grown over, turn left onto a rough dirt road just before the "9" marker nailed to a tree. Continue for another 2.6 km to a small parking area. Your road is obvious until you reach the 2.3 km mark where you fork to the right. The last 100 m is rough and you may wish to park lower down.

| | |
|---|---|
| 0 km | the trailhead |
| 800 m | fork |
| 900 m | Window Mountain Lake |
| 2.9 km | circuit around the lake |
| 3.8 km | return to trailhead |

*Window Mountain Lake below Mount Ward. Photo Tony Daffern.*

## The Window

An interesting geological feature often found throughout the Canadian Rockies is "windows" in mountains. Geologists are not sure what causes such "windows." One theory is that windows were created by erosion along the lines of a joint that caused the block of limestone to pop out. The edges of this window have been rounded and softened by subsequent erosion.

*In the window above Window Mountain Lake, Labour Day weekend, 1933. Left to right: Anne Yuill, Isadore Raymond, Maureen Cooke (Lowe), Esther Taymond (Ash). Photo Edna Morris Ondrus. Courtesy Maureen Lowe.*

## Allison Peak

**Previous Names** The Needles' Eye Window Mountain

Descriptive names such as "The Needles' Eye" and "Window Mountain" were used in the past for this 2643 m-high mountain, and it is still called Window Mountain by local residents today.

However, the official name for the mountain in which the window is found is Allison Peak. It is named for Douglas Allison, an ex-Royal North West Mounted policeman, who temporarily settled near the base of the mountain.

paintbrushes and daisies. Entering spruce forest, the path climbs up and across the steep flank of the headwall to a gap. Near the top it breaks out of the forest to offer views of South Racehorse Creek valley, Crowsnest Mountain and the Seven Sisters. From the high point the path descends to a fork. Bear right and pass a small slough that quickly dries up in summer. Continue along the path to your destination.

Located to the south and southwest are high rugged mountains with patches of perpetual snow towering over picture-perfect Window Mountain Lake. Rest a moment at one of the picnic sites, then take a walk around the lake. The trail to the right leads to an island that is accessible in late summer when the water levels are usually lower. Past here the path narrows as it passes through tall grasses and over rocky outcrops. At the far end of the lake the path is almost indiscernible through scree at the base of Mount Ward, but once past the scree the trail picks up to lead you back to where you began your circuit.

From the Allison Creek road the window in the mountain entices you. But reaching it is a challenge open to only very proficient and knowledgeable rock scramblers. Although other parties no doubt made the successful climb to the window, the first to be reported in the local newspaper was that of a small group of four men in July 1953. They reported they had to rope together because of ice and snow conditions on the summit.

Return the way you came.

# 19 CROWSNEST MOUNTAIN

**NOTE:** While other publications state the summit can be reached in 3.5 hours, the climb is sufficiently challenging to consume 5 hours one way. And remember, you have to return the way you came, so unless you are technically proficient and very fit, allow plenty of time.

Crowsnest Mountain is the physical symbol of the entire Crowsnest Pass area. No hiker can leave this mountain unchallenged!

If from below the mountain does not look accessible to the average hiker, do not be discouraged. One-armed people and pet dogs have made it to the top. The series of cliffs that appear to make Crowsnest a difficult challenge are in fact deceptive. You actually ascend in a series of steps from one talus slope to another. The mountain's hazards include exposure to wind and bad weather, long stretches of loose scree, and gullies full of loose rock where it is essential to always remain alert. It is best to begin as early in the morning as possible as this can be a hot hike. You may well find that two litres of water on a warm day will not be too much to carry.

From the parking lot, cross a shallow stream and walk south about 100 m. Turn left at the east-west cutline. This is the trail that leads toward Crowsnest Mountain. It is a relatively easy but steady climb through pine and spruce forest underlain with alder and salmonberry bushes. Cross a north-south cutline and continue eastward. One kilometre from the trailhead, a small stream on your left swings to the right, necessitating an easy stream crossing. During wet years, or early in the season, there will be other streams coming off the mountain, but in high summer this is the last water source available to you. A break in the forest offers a fine view of Seven Sisters. Where the path breaks out of the trees onto a large scree slope, it takes a sharp turn to the southeast toward Crowsnest Mountain. If Crowsnest Mountain impresses from the highway, it is awesome from close up. Its magnificent cliffs tower far above, while the jagged teeth of the Seven Sisters march in a line on your left.

**Duration** day

**Distance** 12 km return to trailhead

**Level of Difficulty** Scree slopes and loose rock.

**Maximum Elevation** 2730 m

**Elevation Gain** 1108 m

**Map** Crowsnest 82 G/10

## Access

From Highway 3 drive north on the Allison Creek Road. There are two possible trailheads, both on the east side of the road. The first, 10.5 km from Highway 3, is unsigned but is flagged. The second trailhead can be found 100 m past the first trailhead. There is a turnoff that leads to an improvised parking area located on a north-south cutline.

| | |
|---|---|
| 0 m | trailhead |
| 100 m | trail |
| 600 m | cutline |
| 1.0 km | stream |
| 3.0 km | first weeping wall |
| 6.0 km | summit |
| 12.0 km | trailhead |

*Crowsnest Mountain, showing route of ascent up the north face. Photo Tony Daffern.*

The path over the scree to the base of the first set of cliffs is well marked by red surveyor's tape. It is steeper here and the loose scree makes hiking much more difficult. Near the base of the first cliff, the path branches into several alternative routes. Head toward a weeping wall that from the bottom of the scree slope looks like a black chimney against the grey rock. The black is caused by algae marking the presence of a weeping wall even if the water is no longer present. This is a popular rest spot before tackling the mountain proper. Novice hikers or scramblers are advised to turn back at this point if unsure of the route or uncomfortable on steep slopes.

From the weeping wall, follow the base of the cliff to the right, then climb up scree and rock toward a notch at the top of a wide, shallow gully. Twenty metres below the notch the route veers sharply to the left. Your target is a small promontory topped by a pin and red ribbon. (There is an old trail over the notch, down the other side, along the cliff face to a narrow chute. This chute becomes steeper as it nears the top and is now used as an alternate ascent route only by more adventurous or lost souls.)

From the promontory, the trail veers right toward a second cliff and a second weeping wall at the top of the next scree slope. During wet years a high waterfall and stream run all the way down to the first weeping wall. From here, continue left below the cliff toward a third weeping wall and the bottom of a narrow gully. This gully is about 70 m long and filled with heavy gravel topped by loose rocks and scree. Hikers should go up this chute one at a time. From a fork about 30 m from the top, it is a moderately difficult rock scramble up the left fork onto the scree slope above. A pin has been hammered into the rock 10 m from the top. Some hikers use this to secure a rope but, over time, any pin hammered into a rock will loosen.

The main challenges are over; the scree slope beyond has a moderate slope and the trail is wide and well-packed. From the top of the gully, the trail begins a leisurely climb toward the now visible summit. From time to time, there are small cairns with red ribbons marking the way, but the route is always obvious. At a fork about two-thirds of the way up, bear to the left on the less steeper route. It is best to stay on the trail as some of the scree slopes crossed by the trail are very active.

At the summit there are three markers. The centre marker has a canister attached with a sheet of paper and pen where all are invited to sign their name and date of their climb. When the notepad is full of names, it is replaced and the full notepad is taken down to the Crowsnest Museum in Coleman. This is a modern version of a miners' ritual from the early years. To prove they had made the climb, miners lit their miner's lamps and planted them on the summit so they could be seen from below at night.

Located near the third marker, roughly shaped like a cross, is a shallow depression surrounded by a low man-made wall. On windy days this is about the only spot where a leisurely lunch can be enjoyed.

The trip back down to the parking lot usually takes several hours. Be careful. Crowsnest Mountain is a very popular hike and it is not unusual to see a dozen people at various stages in climbing the mountain. Take care not to trigger loose rock down onto someone's head.

*The Seven Sisters from the first weeping wall.*

## Crowsnest Mountain

Perhaps because it stands alone between the High Rock and Livingstone ranges and has long sloping flanks, Crowsnest Mountain is often mistaken for an ancient volcano. In fact, this is not the case. Crowsnest Mountain is actually an isolated remnant of the High Rock Range farther to the west. In other words, at one time, Crowsnest Mountain and Seven Sisters were once continuous with the High Rock Range. Geologists call this geological formation a klippe. Erosion by early glaciers and later by running water has cut through the overlying limestone into the softer rock creating the valley of Allison Creek.

Look at Crowsnest Mountain and you can see the prominent bedding of the grey limestone with its castellated appearance on the upper part of the mountain. The lower part of the mountain is comprised of softer, younger sandstones and shales. Separating the sandstones and shales from the limestone is the Lewis Thrust Fault. For a description of thrust faults, a common occurrence in the Canadian Rockies, see "Along the Livingstone Ridge" hike.

## Reaching the Summit

Crowsnest Mountain was declared to be "attractive to an alpinist" by none other than Edward Whymper, the famous mountaineer who was the first to successfully climb the Matterhorn in Switzerland in 1865. Whymper had been hired in 1901 by the Canadian Pacific Railway, which was anxious to have identified potential tourist attractions along its mainline through Banff. To that end, Whymper was to conduct a survey, map trails and propose roads for the entire route from Banff westward over the Divide. In 1903, Whymper's contract was extended to include the Crowsnest Pass. Although Whymper made his first foray through the pass in September that year, it wasn't until the following year that he returned to explore the tourist possibilities offered by the pass.

Whymper hired Tom Wilson, a well-known Banff guide, and two Swiss guides, Christian Hasler and Friedrich Michel, to cut a trail around Crowsnest Mountain. Whymper gave Wilson instructions not to climb the peak but to report back to him once the trail had been blazed. Much to his annoyance, Whymper received a telegram from Wilson stating he and

*Final gully through cliffbands of Crowsnest Mountain. Photo Gillean Daffern.*

the Swiss guides had climbed Crowsnest Mountain on July 28, two days earlier, and had raised a flag on its summit. When the four men met to discuss cutting a trail around the mountain, the guides asked that Whymper supply them with a bottle of brandy. Now, Whymper had a reputation for being a difficult, inflexible and irasicble man. A penny-pincher to boot and still annoyed that the three had acted on their own, Whymper refused. Imagine his anger when he realized Wilson simply took a bottle and charged it to him! This "very troublesome day" ended in a camp on the west side of Crowsnest Mountain with Wilson, Hasler and Michel enjoying the brandy before retiring to their tents, leaving the clean-up to Whymper and the cook.

The route of that first ascent in 1904 by Tom Wilson and two Swiss guides is unknown. The following year, P. D. McTavish, George Harrower, L. Stauffer and Keith Whimster climbed the mountain's northwest ridge, a difficult route owing to a series of gullies that made progress slow and hazardous. After having left Coleman at 2:00 a.m. they gained the summit at noon "a most jubilant party. Here we found the cairn of rock left by Mr. Wilson's party, but being very amateurish, we failed to examine the glass jar in its centre, which Mr. Wilson subsequently informed me was there, and which contained the name of the former party. The remnants of an old flag we captured as our lawful booty and carried off as a souvenir, leaving in its stead a new one, floating upon the cairn of rock which we erected beside the other."

Lest the reader be left with the impression that mountaineering was a solely male sport at the turn of the century, women were as keen alpinists as the men. Laura Marshall and Helen Hatch were the first two women to reach the summit of Crowsnest Mountain on August 20, 1907. The present route up the north face was first completed by local rancher, F. W. Godsal, in 1915.

# 20 THE MILL RUN

Chinook Lake campground is the nucleus of a series of cross-country ski trails, the Mill Run being one such trail. So named for the road on which logs were skidded out, the Mill Run is a short, pleasant after-dinner walk that loops through the remains of a lumber camp associated with the McLaren Lumber Company.

The trail begins behind campsite No. 45. Walk uphill about 20 m to a fork, bear left and go through a gate. The first viewpoint of Crowsnest Mountain and the Seven Sisters is but a short distance up the trail. Turn left at another fork. At the first T-junction, go right. At the next T-junction, turn left and switchback uphill to another viewpoint of Crowsnest Mountain and Mount Tecumseh. At the junction with Cabin trail cross-country ski trail, bear right and begin climbing toward the High Rock Range. Continue straight ahead at a crossroads with the Cutline trail and arrive at yet another T-junction. Turn left here and walk into an open field marking the site of the camp of the McLaren Lumber Company. By continuing through the clearing, you find a dilapidated log cabin and an old garbage dump.

**Duration** 1 hour

**Distance** 3 km return

**Level of Difficulty** Easy walk on old roads.

**Maximum Elevation** 1585 m

**Elevation Gain** 122 m

**Map** Crowsnest 82 G/10

## Access

Drive 3 km north of Highway 3 on the Allison Creek road. At the junction turn left for the Chinook Lake campground. The trailhead begins at campsite No. 45 to the left of the road.

0 m trailhead
20 m fork
80 m gate

*Mount Tecumseh and cabin near trailhead, ca. 1951. Courtesy Provincial Archives of Alberta, Public Affairs Bureau Collection PA 444/6.*

Swing to the left through the clearing to regain the old logging road. It has been blocked to vehicular traffic, which makes it easier to walk along than many other old roads. Situated halfway along this old road is a marked viewpoint of Mount Tecumseh. The logging road eventually leads back to the washrooms at the opposite end of the campground from the trailhead.

| | |
|---|---|
| 300 m | fork |
| 400 m | T-junction |
| 500 m | T-junction |
| 800 m | junction with Cabin trail |
| 1.2 km | T-junction |
| 2.2 km | viewpoint |
| 3.0 km | campground |

## Mount Tecumseh

**Previous Name** Longfellow

Edward Whymper, famous alpinist, was working for the Canadian Pacific Railway in 1904 when he first suggested the name "Longfellow" for the peak with a long summit ridge west of Crowsnest Mountain. The profile of the mountain reminded Whymper of "the forest primeval bearded with moss." The name does not appear to have gained any local recognition.

In 1957 the name "Mount Tecumseh" was officially given to this 2549 m-high mountain of the High Rock Range. Tecumseh was a Shawnee chief who fled to Canada following an American victory at the battle of Tippecanoe, Indiana. He took his revenge against his old enemies during the War of 1812 when he and his tribe fought for the British against the Americans. He died in the Battle of Moravian Town in Upper Canada in 1813.

## McLaren Lumber Company

Logging was an important industry in the Crowsnest Pass from as early as the late 1890s until the 1950s. There were a number of lumber companies that operated in the pass but probably the largest, and certainly the first, was the McLaren Lumber Company. Senator Peter McLaren of Buckingham, Quebec, was a lumber baron from the Ottawa River valley who was casting about to expand his empire. In 1881, with the west just opening up to cattle ranching and railway construction, Senator McLaren took over an economically troubled sawmill on Mill Creek south of the pass. When Canadian Pacific built its Crowsnest rail line in 1897-1898, he moved the mill some 15 km north of the pass so he could access timber adequate for railway ties and bridge timbers. A few years later, in 1902, he built a new sawmill west of Blairmore at a village called Mountain Mill. In addition to the Canadian Pacific Railway, McLaren also found ready markets in the new towns of the pass and in the mines where all mine entries and roofs of the miners' "rooms" had to be shored up with timbers. A secure roof was important, for rock falls could cause serious injury and worse, dust explosions. To supply his sawmill, McLaren established a number of winter logging camps where he employed some 200 men cutting timbers, which were floated down the rivers when spring arrived. When McLaren's original steam mill burnt down in 1917, he rebuilt west of Blairmore on the Crowsnest River and continued to log the Allison Creek watershed for fir, spruce and lodgepole pine. In 1932, the company ceased operations.

The lumber camp you walked through along The Mill Run was one of those lumber camps.

# 21 DEAD MANS PASS

**Duration** day
**Distance** 15 km return
**Level of Difficulty** Easy walk on hard-packed road.
**Maximum Elevation** 1585 m
**Elevation Gain** 122 m
**Map** Crowsnest 82 G/10

## Access

Drive 3 km north of Highway 3 on the signed Allison Creek road west of Coleman. At the junction turn left for Chinook Lake campground. At the entrances into the campground follow the signs for Dead Mans Pass that take you down a steep hill to Chinook Lake where you can park your vehicle. The signed trail starts from the western edge of the lake just behind the cookhouse.

| | |
|---|---|
| 0 m | trailhead |
| 800 m | stream |
| 1.1 km | fork |
| 2.9 km | junction with old road |
| 3.0 km | fork |
| 3.2 km | remains of lumber camp |
| 5.2 km | eastern edge of pass |
| 7.5 km | western edge of pass |
| 15.0 km | return to trailhead |

All the trails radiating from the campground, including Dead Mans Pass trail, were surveyed and cleared in 1972 for the Alberta Winter Games hosted by the Municipality of Crowsnest Pass. Used in the summer as hiking and biking trails, they double as cross-country ski trails in the winter.

Do not let the name "Dead Mans" fool you; this hike is a delight. Amateur botanists will keep busy identifying the many different species of flowers and vegetation as it changes from lush rainforest to dry alpine meadows.

The splash of colour begins immediately along the lake's edge where salmonberries, cow parsnip, queen's cup, woolly cotton grass and wild strawberries line the path. Leaving the lake, the trail passes through a mixed evergreen forest until reaching a small clearing. Cross a well-made footbridge over the stream. The trail beyond this point narrows and becomes somewhat boggy as it skirts a mossy streambed. At a fork in the path bear right to enter a rain forest area. Meadow parsnips with their yellow clustered flower heads, stately purple/blue lupines, dainty forget-me-nots, fragrant bronze bells and white geraniums, and huge salmonberry bushes are among the plants that nearly obliterate the path.

At 2.9 km bear left onto an old road. The vegetation begins to change after this intersection, the luxurious flora giving way to a mixed forest of pine, spruce and poplar. At a fork in the road keep to the right. From here it is 2 km to the eastern edge of the pass. Beside a small lake are the remains of an old lumber camp established probably by the McLaren Lumber Company. By poking through the long grass you can locate a community dump and wagon parts at the east end of the lake, while a root cellar and derelict log building can be investigated at the west end. This was probably a sawmill camp where men lived, sometimes year round, cutting timber needed for the mill.

*Crowsnest Mountain from the trailhead at Chinook Lake, 1965. Courtesy Provincial Archives of Alberta, Public Affairs Bureau Collection PA 358/2.*

Continue straight along the road, ignoring all seismic cutlines and other old roads. After you leave the lake the vegetation changes to dense alder lining the path and is reminiscent of an old English country lane. Once you break out into the open scree slopes of the High Rock Range, it is somewhat difficult to ascertain the top of the pass as the elevation gain along the final part of the route is so gradual and the pass stretches for 2.5 km.

To reach the Continental Divide, take the right fork where the trail splits and at the top of a small rise view Mount Erikson in British Columbia.

Return the way you came.

## Dead Mans Pass

Dead Mans Pass is an unusual name to give to this charming area. Oral tradition claims 40 U.S. cavalrymen were enticed into this pass by a group of Indians they were chasing. Realizing they were trapped, the cavalry attempted to retreat, but the Indians blocked their path to safety and slaughtered all 40 of the cavalry.

*Unnamed peak in High Rock Range from lumber camp.*

# The Great Divide Trail

*The Great Divide Trail Vision: A sinuous pathway paralleling and crossing the continental divide between Waterton Lakes and Banff national parks, providing opportunities for personal discovery and appreciation of western Canadian heritage through traditional travel by foot and horse.*

TrailNet News July 1999

The Great Divide Trail, 560 km long and running from the American border to Mount Robson Provincial Park, was envisioned in the 1970s as a long distance hiking/equestrian trail. Using existing trails and old roads as much as possible, the Great Divide Trail was to be the main trail along the Continental Divide from which would radiate a network of trails throughout the Forest Reserves in Alberta and British Columbia. The trail through the Crowsnest Pass came from the south along Willoughby Ridge and York Creek into Coleman. From there, it went north along the McGillivray Creek road, swinging west along a power transmission line to the Allison Creek road. From here, it went along the Allison Creek road and then swung over to Dead Mans Pass trail from where it dropped down to Alexander Creek in British Columbia.

The Alberta government initially supported the Great Divide Trail with grants to help with trail construction and with protection from incompatible uses such as ATVs, trail bikes and industry. Even industry supported the original vision. But in the late 1980s government policy changed. The ban on ATVs and trail bikes was lifted, resulting in serious erosion of the trail. Likewise, the government granted logging concerns permits adjacent to the trail. Faced with such disheartening circumstances, volunteers drifted away and the Great Divide Trail Association ceased to exist. Recently, though, some of the original members are reviving the idea of a Great Divide Trail. But much work will be needed to repair bridges washed out and to clean out debris caused by the 1995 flood.

The concept of the GDT has recently been revived in a book, *Hiking Canada's Great Divide Trail* by Dustin Lynx and published by Rocky Mountain Books in 2000.

# 22 CHINOOK LAKE LOOP

A pleasant stroll along the lake's edge is a relaxing way to either end or begin your day. This is a walk the whole family can enjoy.

From the bottom of the hill, walk across the parking area and go down to the lake. A good walking path appears close to the lake's edge. Turn right and follow it as it leaves the open area for the cool forest where you can find an understorey of strawberries and mosses. Steps take you down the steeper slopes as you swing around the east end of the lake. If you wish to enjoy the view from higher ground, go right at a fork that appears in the trail. It leads to a bench and a viewpoint that takes in the High Rock Range. Return to the main path and bear to the right along the path that now descends to the lake's outflow. Cross a bridge over a concrete sluice and keep to the left on the other side to continue your loop around Chinook Lake. Poisonous horsetails can be found alongside the path that now crosses a marsh. Don't worry about wet shoes; a boardwalk has been laid across the wet areas for you.

Once past the boardwalk, the vegetation changes abruptly. Whereas dank forest was found on the north-facing slope, here on the south-facing slope you can find scented prickly wild roses, ground-hugging kinnikinnick, purple harebells and junipers, all of which prefer open sunny locations. As you approach the west end of the lake, the vegetation changes once again as you skirt the swampy in-flow of an unnamed creek. As you reenter the open forest you can find several gnawed stumps of spruce trees, evidence of the presence of the industrious beaver. Although beavers normally prefer poplar, in this instance they seem to have settled for spruce!

The path now swings to the left, crossing the creek by means of a good log bridge. One hundred metres later the path ends at a T-junction with Dead Mans Pass trail. Turn left and follow the wide path back to the parking lot.

**Duration** 1 hour
**Distance** 3 km
**Level of Difficulty** Easy walk along good trail and boardwalk.
**Maximum Elevation** 1463 m
**Elevation Gain** negligible
**Map** Crowsnest 82 G/10

## Access

Drive 3 km north of Highway 3 on the signed Allison Creek road west of Coleman. At the junction turn left for Chinook Lake campground and descend a steep hill to Chinook Lake where you can park your vehicle.

| | |
|---|---|
| 0 m | trailhead |
| 500 m | fork |
| 600 m | sluice |
| 2.1 km | T-junction |
| 3.0 km | return to trailhead |

# Sentinel

**Previous Name** Sentry Siding

The name "Sentry Siding" referred to the railway siding established here in 1909. It may have been that the siding was named "Sentry" after a prominent mountain nearby. Why the name of the siding and hamlet was changed to "Sentinel" is unknown.

Picturesquely located at the east end of Crowsnest Lake tucked beneath the peaks of the High Rock Range lies the hamlet of Sentinel, a quiet village of perhaps 100 souls.

While Sentinel is the first known permanent settlement on Crowsnest Lake, the lake was the scene of seasonal hunting and fishing camps for thousands of years. Archaeologists have discovered a major prehistoric campsite nearby that spans some 4,000 years of occupation. Peoples of the Mummy Cave culture first camped here some 8,000 years ago, returning over the millennia each summer to hunt and fish.

In more recent times, Sentinel began in 1909 as a railway siding, called Sentry Siding, where livestock and clay for the brickworks in Medicine Hat were loaded into waiting rail cars. Sentinel received a boost in 1924 when East Kootenay Power built a steam generating hydroelectric plant on Crowsnest Lake. The plant and the coal mines quickly formed a symbiotic relationship. East Kootenay Power purchased powdered coal that had no commercial value from the pass mines and used it to fire its boilers. As the plant consumed 200 tons of coal daily, it was equally a boon to the mining industry that now had a market for its otherwise worthless powdered coal. The powdered coal was blown into the fire boxes and burned in suspension, most of the residue being carried up the 52 m smokestack. First considered an auxiliary plant, the East Kootenay Power plant was soon generating electricity for the pass full time. Many of the power plant's employees took up residence near the railway siding, thus creating the hamlet of Sentinel. The most "complete supersteam plant in Alberta" closed in February, 1969, when Calgary Power bought out all the East Kootenay Power plants in Alberta. Sentinel reverted to its quiet solitude.

The economy of the Crowsnest Pass depended heavily on the fortunes of the coal industry. Fluctuations in the world and Canadian markets, strikes and shortages of rail cars resulted in a volatile local economy. To offset the dependency on coal, a number of enterprises sprang up before the First World War. One of these was the quarrying of limestone. Used primarily in the mortar of brick and as a constituent of cement, the limestone deposits in the pass make quarrying a profitable business. It all started at the turn of the 20th century when E. G. Hazell, on hearing that this limestone deposit could produce a plastic lime that spread easily with a trowel, purchased the business from two men who had first exploited these deposits. For nearly a century, the Hazell family and its Summit Lime Works Ltd. have supplied western Canada and northwest United States with calcium lime. In contrast to the quarry of the Summit Lime Works are the limestone deposits across Highway 3. An old quarry that had been closed for a number of years was reactivated for riprap for the Oldman Dam.

Over the years, several entrepreneurs have tried to attract local residents and railway passengers to Crowsnest, Island and Emerald Lake, located on the other side of Highway 3. In 1915, for instance, a passenger boat took tours around Crowsnest Lake on Sundays and, in 1930, A. Morency built a dancing pavilion and cabins here, but all attempts to sustain a brisk tourist trade failed. Only the Glacier Cabins built in the late 1940s along the west shore of Crowsnest Lake have survived under the current name Kozy Knest Kabins.

# 23 CROWSNEST LAKE

An easy walk, this hike makes a circuit of Crowsnest Lake. En route you visit a locally famous cave believed at one time to be the source of the Oldman River and that offers both recent and historical graffiti and Indian rock paintings.

**Duration** 2 hours

**Distance** 7.3 km return

**Level of Difficulty** Easy walk along a path, railway track and paved road.

**Maximum Elevation** 1372 m

**Elevation Gain** negligible

**Map** Crowsnest 82 G/10

## Access

Park at the Crowsnest Lake Information Centre kiosk at the west end of Crowsnest Lake on Highway 3 west of Coleman.

| | |
|---|---|
| 0 m | trailhead |
| 500 m | railway track |
| 1.5 km | cave |
| 4.5 km | Sentinel |
| 7.3 km | return to the Information Centre |

From the interpretive signs take the path that skirts around the western margin of the lake, bypassing a summer camp. Reputedly one of the deepest lakes in the province, Crowsnest Lake provides sanctuary to ducks, geese and swans, all of which you might see as you walk along the lake's edge. At the end of the lake scramble up to the mainline of the Canadian Pacific Railway, then head east along the railway right-of-way, checking behind you now and then for any trains.

Approximately halfway along the lake you arrive opposite a cave. A short path leads down to the stream issuing from its mouth. A somewhat hazardous scramble over smooth and sometimes slippery rock leads to the cave entrance. In the spring and early summer the volume of water

*Overlooking the lake, 1951. Courtesy Provincial Archives of Alberta, Public Affairs Bureau Collection PA 444/10.*

## The Canadian Pacific Railway

It was the construction of the Canadian Pacific Railway through the Crowsnest Pass in 1897-98 that opened the pass to settlement and to the exploitation of the area's natural resources. Bituminous coal was needed by the new and expanding smelting industries of southeast British Columbia. Hiring some 4,000 men, the Canadian Pacific decided to run its most southerly line from Lethbridge to Kootenay Lake in British Columbia. Construction began in July 1897 and was completed in August of the next year—very fast considering the mountainous terrain they had to surmount. But not all went smoothly. A cholera epidemic swept through the construction camp while it was working on the line just on the west side of the Divide. A large percentage of the labourers were Chinese who had worked on the construction of the main line in the late 1870s and early 1880s. Many of them succumbed to the disease and were buried at a site nearby. The Crow's Nest Pass Coal Company began immediately to develop coal deposits on the west side of the pass while the future development of coal resources on the eastern side of the pass was assured by the railway. The Canadian Pacific Railway needed coal, and lots of it, to fire its steam engines from the coast over the Continental Divide and across the prairies to eastern Canada. It was pass coal that freed the railway company from buying expensive Pennsylvania coal.

The creation of the Rocky Mountains Park, now Banff National Park, in 1885 opened the Canadian Rockies to a new breed of train traveller—the tourist. Quick to understand the potential of this new trend, the Canadian Pacific Railway undertook the construction of major hotels at choice locations along its route. Shortly after the construction of the Crowsnest line, the railway company hired the famous mountaineer, Edward Whymper, to seek out, among other things, possible locations for new hotel sites. When Whymper visited the Crowsnest Pass in 1904, he became enchanted with Crowsnest Lake and its island, which he felt was an ideal location for a railway chalet or hotel. Besides its picturesque location, the hotel was close to a cave (which you visited on your hike). In his mind's eye, Whymper saw a bathhouse built next to the cave's mouth with steps cut out of the rock to make its interior accessible to visitors. Needless to say, neither idea was carried forward.

gushing from the cave is substantial and can be seen from the highway. In late summer and early autumn this flow is normally reduced to a trickle, unless it has been raining hard, thus making access into the cave possible. The names of earlier adventurers line the walls near the mouth, and farther back green and black Indian paintings can be discerned. Please do not mark these prehistoric images. Rock art is rare in Alberta and these paintings represent a resource forever lost should they be destroyed.

From the cave, continue east along the railway right-of-way past the abandoned East Kootenay Power plant. At the level railway crossing, take the road into Sentinel and follow the main gravel road out of Sentinel back to Highway 3. Then walk west to your vehicle.

*The cave, ca. 1940. Courtesy Provincial Archives of Alberta, Harry Pollard Collection P 4746.*

## The Cave

The Front Ranges of the Rocky Mountains are composed primarily of carbonates, one variety of which is limestone. Where there is limestone, there are often caves. Caves are formed from the dissolving of the limestone by slightly acidic groundwater. In the case of the Crowsnest Lake cave, acidic groundwater has percolated along the Lewis Thrust Fault. This fault is exposed at the base of the hill. Where the acidic groundwater emerges, it has dissolved the rock to form this cave.

A commission sent to delineate the boundary between Alberta and British Columbia in 1916 speculated whether or not the subterranean stream was in part fed from Phillipps Lake at the summit of Phillipps Pass directly north of you. The commissioners, though, could not agree.

# 24 RUMRUNNER'S RUN

This easy walk along an old roadway that crosses over the Continental Divide offers you a chance to relive the days of Prohibition when the sale of alcohol was banned in Alberta.

From the interpretive signs, walk to the west end of the parking lot and pick up the gravel road as it swings around behind the field where the interpretive signs are located. Ignore an old track on the right and follow the road to its end at the base of a hill where there is an intersection of three tracks. The Rumrunner's Run trail is the centre track leading up the hill in front of you through stands of lodgepole pine. It is a steady climb to the top of Phillipps Pass. Take a break occasionally to pause and look back toward British Columbia and the mountain ranges on the western horizon. Near the top of the pass the old road joins a newer, roughly-gravelled road leading to a microwave tower. For a spectacular view of the entire length of the Crowsnest Pass on the Alberta side, it is worth hiking the extra 3.5 km up the switchbacks to the microwave transmitter tower on the top of Crowsnest Ridge. Transmitters of long distance telephone and television intercommunication, microwave towers are built approximately 50 km apart, the limit that wavelengths can travel owing to the curvature of the earth. The construction of this tower was both costly and time consuming. The rocky slope had to be blasted so that the road you are walking on could be built. Also, high winds often prevented crews from working much past mid-morning. Immediately below the ridge are Island, Crowsnest and Emerald lakes, the Island Lake campground and the quarry of the Summit Lime works.

Return to the Phillipps Pass road and continue eastward. Above and out of sight on your left is Mount Phillipps, which is actually the west peak of Mount Tecumseh. Shortly beyond the intersection is a sink hole to the right named Phillipps Lake. The fact that Phillipps Lake does not have an observable outlet created considerable problems for the Boundary Commission, which, in 1914, was delineating the boundary between Alberta and

**Duration** half day
**Distance** 10.5 km
**Level of Difficulty** Easy walk on hard-packed road.
**Maximum Elevation** 1555 m
**Elevation Gain** 183 m
**Map** Crowsnest 82 G/10

## Access

This hike requires two vehicles. Park your first vehicle at the Canadian Pacific Railway tracks in Sentinel.

Then drive your second vehicle to the Crowsnest Rest Area, British Columbia, which is located 1 km west of the boundary viewpoint. Park your vehicle by the interpretive panels located adjacent to the parking lot.

| | |
|---|---|
| 0 m | trailhead at Crowsnest Rest Area, British Columbia |
| 200 m | intersection of three tracks |
| 2.2 km | intersection with new gravel road |
| 5.7 km | microwave tower |
| 10.5 km | Sentinel, Alberta |

British Columbia along the Continental Divide. Some members of the commission theorized the water drained underground, surfacing again at the cave entry along Crowsnest Lake (see Crowsnest Lake hike on page 89). But the British Columbia commissioners disagreed with their Alberta and federal contemporaries with the result that the question was allowed to rest for a while. Finally, the boundary line was placed across the centre of the tarn giving each province half of the area.

Located just past the lake is a concrete block marking the provincial boundary. These were placed every 1.6 to 4.8 km along the length of the Divide. There are a couple of braids in the road but they soon all rejoin. The hike ends at the Canadian Pacific Railway crossing in Sentinel where you have parked your first vehicle.

*Alberta Provincial Police searching for liquor near Coleman. Courtesy Provincial Archives of Alberta, Archives Collection A 4793.*

## The Rumrunners

Today, the first wagon road built through Crowsnest Pass offers an uneventful walk. But not during the first decades of the 20th century when Phillipps Pass witnessed numerous rumrunners carrying illicit liquor from British Columbia into Coleman, Blairmore, Hillcrest and Bellevue. "Blind pigs" selling bootleg whiskey were both popular and numerous. This was especially true after 1916 when Alberta voted to restrict the sale and consumption of alcoholic beverages. Prohibition was popular among supporters of the temperance movement but not among many of the general populace and illegal stills churning out moonshine and "blind pigs" or "speakeasies" carried out their business, often openly defying the law. The difficulties of regulating the law eventually brought about the lifting of Prohibition in 1923.

The days of Prohibition offer some of the more exciting dramas in Alberta history. One of the most successful rumrunners was Emilio Picariello, or as he was affectionately named, Emperor Pick. He owned the Alberta Hotel in Blairmore, which fronted for a "blind pig." Using a Model-T Ford with concrete-filled pipe bumpers, the Emperor ran liquor across Phillipps Pass for several years. To the constant chagrin of the newly formed Alberta Provincial Police, the Emperor and his son slipped through every roadblock and trap they set—except the last one. Tipped off one night that the Emperor's son was running a carload of booze into the pass, the police gave chase. It ended in downtown Coleman where the son was injured during a shoot-out. The Emperor, hearing that his son had been killed, tore into town with a companion, Florence Lassandro. In a confrontation with Constable Lawson, the officer was killed and Picariello and Lassandro were both charged with murder. Now, to that date no woman had been hanged in Alberta. At the trial Lassandro was identified as having pulled the trigger in the hope that both would be acquitted. Nevertheless, both of the accused ended their days on the gallows. To this day, Lassandro remains the only woman to be hanged in the province.

## Phillipps Pass

Phillipps Pass is named after Michael Phillipps, a Hudson's Bay Company clerk who first recorded this pass and the outcroppings of coal through the area in 1860. Later in 1879, he constructed the first trail across this 1550 m-high pass. Michael Phillipps died in 1916 and his name was officially given to this most northerly of the Crowsnest system of passes in 1959.

## The Great Train Robbery

Sentinel made newspaper headlines in August 1920. On the second of that month, three men, Tom Bassoff, George Arkoff and Aubey Arloff, boarded the express train in the village thinking that the local rumrunner, Emilio Picariello, was on board with a large amount of cash. Although they did not find Picariello, the three robbed the rest of the passengers in this the first and to date, the last train robbery to take place in the Crowsnest Pass. Five days later, police were tipped off the two "desperate looking characters answering the description of the bandits" were in the Bellevue Cafe, a local Chinese restaurant. The arrival of three Alberta Provincial Police officers shortly afterward resulted in a bloody shoot-out that left Arkoff and two officers dead. Bassoff and Arloff escaped but were eventually captured. Bassoff's career ended on the gallows, Arloff's in prison.

# The Flatheads

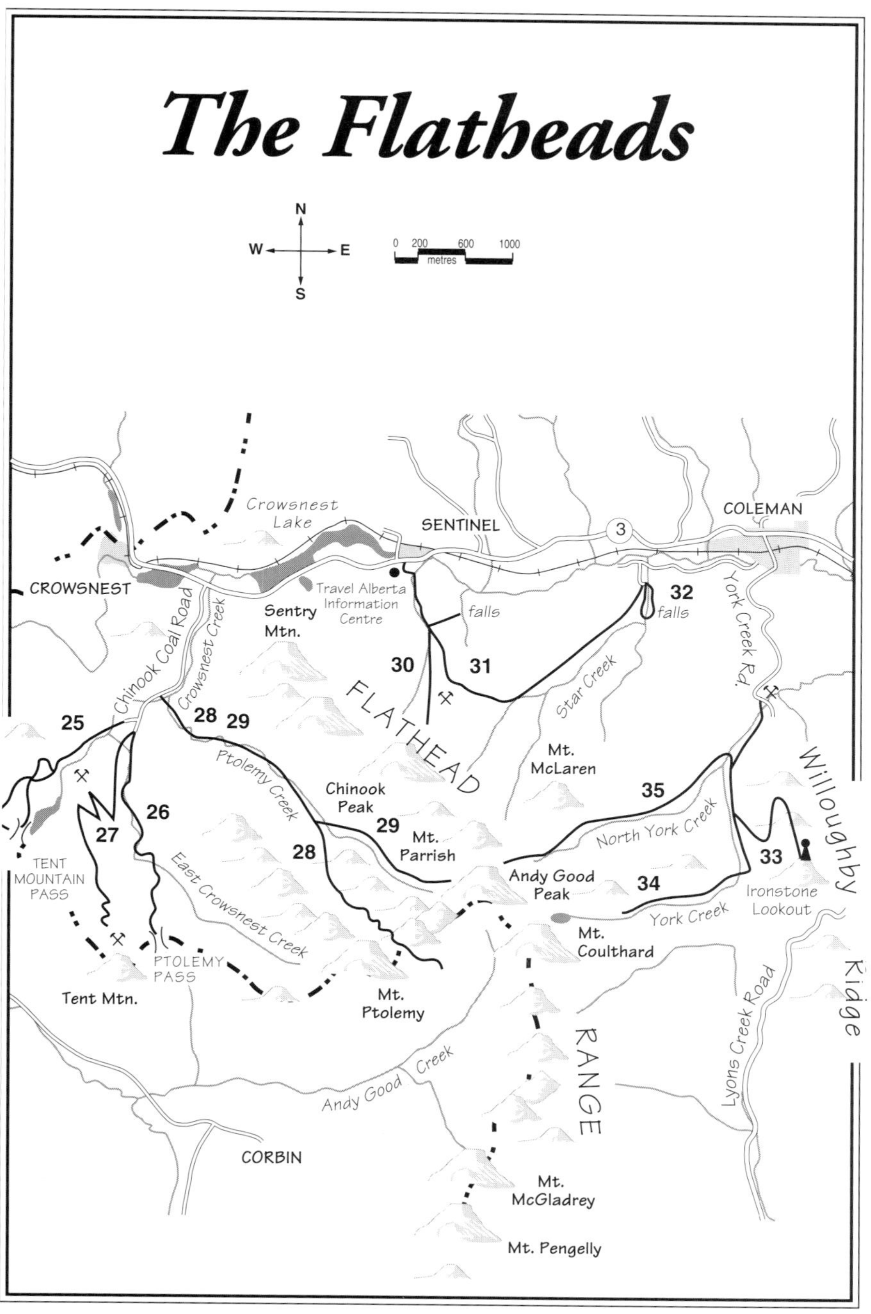

# Crowsnest

When you are heading west into British Columbia on Highway 3 it's easy to miss the hamlet of Crowsnest. But, as you are driving over Summit Pass, pull over to a viewpoint and there below, tucked between the railway tracks and the mountain, you can see the Inn On the Border, a bed and breakfast establishment marking the approximate location of Crowsnest.

Straddling the Alberta/British Columbia border, Crowsnest was established in the late 1890s when the Canadian Pacific Railway was pushing its line through to Kootenay Lake in British Columbia. Later, the hamlet took on a greater significance when the railway made Crowsnest a divisional point along its line. Although other enterprises employed a few people, the train remained the life line of the village. In the 1920s, the westbound passenger train arrived at 10:30 p.m. while the eastbound train arrived the next morning at 9:30 a.m. Later, in the 1930s, the number of passenger trains was reduced to three times a week, but they continued to stop at Crowsnest for a 20 minute break so the passengers could stretch their legs and the crews could change.

Never boasting more than 200 people, Crowsnest could only brag of six houses, three located on either side of the railway tracks, a railway station, a boarding house for the crews, a bunkhouse, the round house for the train engines, a laundry, post office, general store and a Presbyterian church that doubled as a school and, when called upon, the local dance hall! The railway built three more houses for its family men in the 1920s and there were several other log houses that stretched along the narrow valley. No village or town is ever without its hotel and Crowsnest had the Summit Hotel. The original building was located behind the present establishment, the proprietor of which was Andy Good, a prospector and hunter who displayed trophy game heads in his bar and lobby to an admiring clientele.

Today, little remains of the village. A walk along the old roadway reveals depressions and cellars indicating where the buildings once stood.

*CPR crew at the Summit Hotel. Courtesy Glenbow Archives, NA 1384-3.*

# 25 TENT MOUNTAIN PASS

Tent Mountain Pass is one of several passes that penetrate the Rocky Mountains on either side of Highway 3. Although the pass is low—this is neither a strenuous nor a difficult hike—the views from the top offer a fitting conclusion to the tramp. Along the way is an abandoned mine dating from the 1920s.

At the trailhead take the left-hand fork and walk in a generally southerly direction along what used to be a truck road connecting Tent Mountain to Highway 3. Continue along this road as far as a 90 degree bend in the road. Rather than following the road uphill to the right, continue straight ahead along what is now a grassy pathway. This once was

**Duration** half day

**Distance** 7.4 km return

**Level of Difficulty** Easy walk on hard-packed roads and trails. Some bushwhacking.

**Maximum Elevation** 1524 m

**Elevation Gain** 61 m

**Map** Crowsnest 82 G/10

## Access

Drive to the unsigned Chinook Coal road that lies 4.78 km west of the Travel Information Centre on Highway 3 west of Coleman. Follow the road for 4.5 km to the locked security gate. Just before the gate, drive up a road to the right. At a fork take the left-hand road to yet another fork and park.

| | |
|---|---|
| 0 m | trailhead |
| 1.4 km | old rail bed |
| 1.9 km | Boulton Prospect No. 2 |
| 3.5 km | fork |
| 3.7 km | viewpoint |
| 7.4 km | return to trailhead |

*Waterfall en route to the trailhead.*

the old rail bed of the Spokane and Alberta Coal & Coke Railway. It is now a wet and marshy trail that supports colour splashes of common yarrow, hairy golden asters, pearly everlastings and buttercups. After a short distance, the rail grade disappears under a beaver pond on Crowsnest Creek. The pond is shallow, allowing the luxuriant growth of marsh grasses. You may be lucky enough to see a moose browsing. The flooded rail bed necessitates a bushwhack along the edge of the pond as far as a pile of coal slack. This signals your arrival at Boulton mining prospect No. 2. Climb the slack and find the mine entry on top. Before leaving the mine site, look over to the other side of the beaver pond where Boulton prospect No. 1 was located at the base of the much later open pit mine on Tent Mountain.

From the slack pile follow a path leading up to an old road bed and follow it south for as far as it goes. As this road serviced only the immediate prospect area it soon peters out, leaving you to bushwhack to the top of the ridge on your right. Cut straight across the old logged area to an old road that is the Tent Mountain pass wagon road built by the British Columbia government a few years after the turn of the 20th century. It follows the route through Crowsnest Pass taken in 1882 and 1883 by George Dawson, a geologist in the employ of the Geological Survey of Canada whose job was to map the passes through the Rocky Mountains.

A number of logging roads intersect at this juncture, take the road that leads straight south toward Tent Mountain pass. Keep to the main road. If in doubt, follow the road that leads down to some lakes that are the headwaters of Crowsnest Creek. At a fork in the road near the Continental Divide, take the right-hand fork that switchbacks up to a viewpoint overlooking the western end of the pass. Below you is the broad sweep of the Michel Creek valley dominated by the high peak of Mount Taylor. Relax and enjoy the view before returning.

To return, continue up the switchbacks to the top of the ridge north of Tent Mountain pass. A game trail heads north along the top of a rocky face. Follow it past the outcrop, then bushwhack down the slope and rejoin Tent Mountain pass wagon road. Turn left and cross the old logged area to a fork in the road. Take the right-hand fork down to the beaver dams and, hence, back to your vehicle.

# 26 PTOLEMY PASS

This is a pleasant, easy hike up the valley of East Crowsnest Creek to a pass on the Continental Divide.

The creek accompanies the road most of the way but requires fording several times. After a little more than 2 km the road forks. Follow the right-hand fork. (The left-hand road simply circles higher up the shoulder of the valley through clear-cut, eventually looping back to the road in 1.5 km.) Beyond this junction the road begins its slow climb to Ptolemy Pass. Five hundred metres later there is another fork. Bear right here for views of the massive workings of Tent Mountain mine across the valley of East Crowsnest Creek. At the next fork take a short detour by heading right to a promontory—an even better viewpoint of the workings.

Today, the scarred sides of Tent Mountain are still visible despite the reclamation of the mountainside by the seeding of the coal slack. As open pit mining both disturbs and totally destroys soil and vegetation, reclamation is a means of restoring the land to a state that it can once again support vegetation. The steep slopes must have made the reclamation of Tent Mountain a challenge.

**Duration** day
**Distance** 12 km return
**Level of Difficulty** Easy walk on a hard-packed road.
**Maximum Elevation** 1616 m
**Elevation Gain** 152 m
**Map** Crowsnest 82 G/10

## Access

Drive to the unsigned Chinook Coal road that lies 4.8 km west of the Travel Information Centre on Highway 3 west of Coleman. Follow the road for 4.5 km to the locked security gate and park. Your trail is the old road leading to the left.

| | |
|---|---|
| 0 m | trailhead |
| 2.1 km | fork |
| 4.1 km | second fork |
| 4.5 km | viewpoint |
| 6.0 km | head of the pass |
| 12.0 km | return to trailhead |

*Mount Ptolemy from Tent Mountain.*

## Mount Ptolemy

**Previous Name** Mummy Mountain

Initially, this mountain was known as Mummy Mountain, named by A. O. Wheeler. Wheeler, who was making a photographic survey of the Crowsnest coal seams for the Dominion government, was seated one day on a ridge opposite the mountain when it occurred to him its profile resembled the bust of a sleeping mummy. However, in 1914 when the Boundary Commission discovered the Continental Divide passed over the mountain, it was decided Mummy Mountain was not dignified enough and the commission suggested the name Ptolemy after an ancient Greek astronomer. Ptolemy was bestowed upon the mountain, the pass and the creek. Mount Ptolemy's highest summit stands at 2813 m and was first conquered in the early 1960s from the British Columbia side.

## The Boundary Commission

Between 1913 and 1924 commissioners representing both Alberta and British Columbia were assigned the task of surveying the Continental Divide as the border between the two provinces. They employed a technique called photo-topography. This, explained A. O. Wheeler, one of the commissioners for British Columbia, "necessitated the taking of photographs from very many high mountain summits, and the locating of such photographic stations and computation of their altitudes above sea level by means of instrumental triangulation and trigonometric levelling." Needless to say, the commissioners had to be keen mountaineers as their work meant they climbed literally hundreds of mountain peaks in their travels between the United States border and the 120th meridian of longitude.

One of the commissioners for Alberta and a Dominion lands surveyor, R. W. Cautley experienced some trouble while surveying the Crowsnest system of passes. It seems as though the resident bear population sensed a change in the air with the commission's arrival and took exception to the invasion of their privacy. Two bears repeatedly tumbled "sacks of cement into the holes dug for the [boundary] monument bases, scattered gravel used for concrete and, on one occasion, dragged a full sack of cement more than a quarter of a mile through the woods"!

Continue along the road. Approximately 1.5 km later you arrive at Ptolemy Pass, the most southerly of the Crowsnest system of passes over the Continental Divide. Here, you can find a cairn on the right that marks the Alberta/British Columbia border. In 1914 the Boundary Commission erected 54 concrete cairns at regular intervals along the Alberta/British Columbia border. This one is numbered 93F, the F denoting the first cairn to be built in the Crowsnest area near the hamlet of Crowsnest. Although the top of the pass is surrounded by forest, you can see Mount Pengelly and Mount McGladrey above the treetops to the southeast.

Return the way you came. (The road continues into British Columbia where it joins Corbin Road.)

# 27 TENT MOUNTAIN

**Duration** day
**Distance** 14.5 km return
**Level of Difficulty** Fairly steep climb on hard-packed road.
**Maximum Elevation** 2134 m
**Elevation Gain** 640 m
**Map** Crowsnest 82 G/10

## Access

Drive to the unsigned Chinook Coal road that lies 4.8 km west of the Travel Information Centre on Highway 3 west of Coleman. Follow the road for 4.5 km to the locked security gate. This is your trailhead.

| | |
|---|---|
| 0 m | trailhead at the security gate |
| 3.9 km | surface plant |
| 6.7 km | saddle |
| 14.5 km | return to the trailhead |

The pull up Tent Mountain across the workings of the last of the coal mines on the Alberta side of the Crowsnest Pass is well worth the effort for the views that greet you from the summit.

Begin this hike by crossing over the locked gate and following the abandoned coal mine road uphill through mixed forest. The most northerly workings of the ruptured mountainside dominate your view of Tent Mountain all the way to the remains of the surface plant. After several switchbacks you reach the base of the actual open pit mine. There is a repair shop, water tower and various outbuildings.

From the surface plant, continue following the road in a southerly direction to the open pit. Mount Ptolemy and the cut face in the mountain created by the open pit mining process form a dramatic backdrop to the pit and "lake" below. The deep pit has not been fenced so do not tempt fate by peering over the edge! The cut reveals two interesting geological features. First, you will notice the thick coal seam and understand how relatively accessible

*Tent Mountain mine, May 3, 1948. Photo Thomas Gushul. Courtesy Glenbow Archives, NC 54-2905.*

Tent Mountain coal was for the mining company. The second feature you will notice is the downward fold of the seam in the worked face. Folding, or the bending of rocks in wave-like formations, is caused by tremendous pressure and heat from below being exerted on the rock above over long periods of time. This particular fold, because it bends downward, is called a syncline.

To gain the top of the mountain behind the open pit is either a long walk via the switchbacking road, or a shorter but steeper scramble straight up the front. When the mine closed in 1983, new environmental controls dictated that the slopes be seeded. The coarse grass makes walking uneven and somewhat difficult. A saddle near the top of the ridge affords fine views of the Crowsnest Pass from east to west.

Return via the same route.

## Open Pit Mining

The British American Coal Company, formed in 1897 to explore the possibilities at the west end of the Crowsnest Pass, was the first of several companies that expressed interest in the coal seams in the Tent Mountain area. Although the company did some prospecting, it did not develop any of its properties and by 1919 sold its leases to an American concern, the Spokane and Alberta Coal & Coke Company. This company opened the Boulton prospects No. 1 and 2 but by 1923 faulted seams and the lack of money forced the closure of the mine. Another company, the Tent Mountain Coal Company, incorporated in 1912 and formed by a group of Calgary businessmen, held leases on Tent Mountain proper. With an authorized capital of $1,000,000, the company began work on a spur rail line and planned a model mining town, one in which drinking establishments and other "vicious resorts" were banned. Most miners preferred to wash the coal dust from their throats in the bars after work. Whether or not this fact combined with the ban on saloons had any bearing on the company's fortunes is not known. However, Tent Mountain Coal Company did not develop the seams beyond opening one or two prospects.

The Tent Mountain coal deposits lay dormant until the late 1940s when Hillcrest-Mohawk Collieries in Bellevue prospected and eventually opened an open pit mine here. By then, modern technology made it possible to strip coal seams. Where coal seams approach the tops of ridges, it is possible to exploit the seams by first removing the overburden of trees, soil and rock. Then the trucks and shovels move in, working down through the seam, thus forming an open pit. Hillcrest-Mohawk Collieries opened the "Glacier Strip" in 1948. Some of the seams such as the one you can see on this hike are very thick. In the mountain building process, great internal pressures caused the rock formations to fold, sometimes at a dizzy 70 degrees. Continual pressures caused the folds to be squeezed together to form thick bands. Hillcrest-Mohawk did not have tipple facilities at Tent Mountain; it was more economical to truck the coal to Bellevue, a distance of 40 km. When Hillcrest-Mohawk and McGillivray International of Coleman amalgamated to form Coleman Collieries, the last company to operate mines on the Alberta side of the Crowsnest Pass, the new company continued stripping the Tent Mountain seams. Failing markets forced the closure of Coleman Collieries and the Tent Mountain mine in 1983.

# The Spokane and Alberta Coal & Coke Company

The Flathead area of the Crowsnest Pass has a chequered mining history. The British American Coal Company, chartered in 1897, was the first to test the coal seams here. But little real mining took place and in 1919 the company began negotiations on the sale of its property to the Spokane and Alberta Coal & Coke Company. American investors were attracted to the company because of an agreement with the Tri State Terminal Association out of the American Pacific northwest. The agreement called for 30,000 tons of coal the first year of production and 100,000 tons in subsequent years. Such promises spurred the Spokane and Alberta Coal & Coke Company to open in that same year the Boulton prospects No. 1 and No. 2. Before going into limbo at the end of 1919, the one entry had pushed 146 m into the hill and the other entry had progressed 192 m.

Work then stalled for two years, perhaps because the agreement with Tri State fell through, and it wasn't until December 1922 that the *Coleman Journal* sang "Something to crow about at Crowsnest." The Spokane and Alberta Coal & Coke Company had restarted its operation with 15 men employed underground and 20 above ground at the tipple. Mine work was not all that the company had to do, though. In order to market its coal, it had to build an 8 km-long spur line from the Canadian Pacific Railway main line to the Boulton mine prospects. A year later the newspaper reported "the spur-line to the mine is practically completed, there being only about 25 feet of rock to blast. At present, there are over 100 men working on the property and there are good prospects for extensive development work being done this spring." But its American backers, discouraged by the failing market and perhaps by the washout of the rail grade by spring floods, decided to abandon their efforts and the rails were never laid. Although sporadic attempts over the next six years were made to revive the mine, they were to no avail.

*Tent Mountain open pit mine. Prior to the commencement of open pit mining here in 1948, the profile of this 2197 m-high mountain was that of a tent, hence the descriptive name. However, frenzied mining on Tent Mountain for more than 30 years totally destroyed the mountain's silhouette.*

# 28 TRAIL TO THE PROMISED LAND

*"He's allowed me to go to the mountain.*
*And I've looked over,*
*and I've seen the promised land."*
Martin Luther King Jr., April 3, 1968

This is truly one of the best hikes the Crowsnest Pass has to offer. The gradual climb from the trailhead to the end of the road with its sneak previews of the Flatheads is only the beginning. It is the tortured landscape of the Andy Good Plateau with its numerous caves and frost pockets located at the top of the Continental Divide that make this hike magnificent.

Owing to the distance involved and the elevation gain, the hike from the trailhead makes too long a day for some people. Remember, you will want to spend several hours exploring the Promised Land. Backpacking into the campsite is recommended. However, if you have a four-wheel-drive vehicle you can use it for the first 6 km. Even then, because the final 1.8 km boasts a 762 m height gain, an early start is recommended.

From the trailhead, the four-wheel-drive road parallels Ptolemy Creek as it leads back into the Flatheads. The road follows a relatively straight course but is forced to cross the rushing waters of the creek eight times. Because the creek can be high in the spring and has a strong current, there are a variety of bridges, which range from mere logs thrown across the creek to more substantial structures. A short distance past the first crossing there is a fork in the road. Continue straight ahead, or to the left.

After the seventh creek crossing the Flathead Range, consisting of Mount Ptolemy, Andy Good and Mount Parrish, comes into full view. Nearly 1 km later, the road heads down a steep hill and crosses Ptolemy Creek for the last time. This is your last chance to fill your canteen. The road now begins to climb more sharply. At a major fork 4.9 km from the trailhead, bear right and trudge along the hard-packed road between dense spruce forest to its end. There is space here to park a vehicle or pitch a tent. If you have hiked from the trailhead a

**Duration** day or backpack

**Distance** 16 km return or 4 km return

**Level of Difficulty** Hard-packed road for first 6 km, then a steep unrelenting climb on trail.

**Maximum Elevation** 2439 m

**Elevation Gain** 1005 m

**Map** Coleman 82 G/10

## Access

Drive to the unsigned Chinook Coal road that lies 4.8 km west of the Travel Alberta Information Centre on Highway 3 west of Coleman. Follow the road for 2.9 km to where the hydro line crosses the road. Pull off to the left and park.

| | |
|---|---|
| 0 m | trailhead and first stream crossing |
| 600 m | fork |
| 1.5 km | second stream crossing |
| 1.7 km | third stream crossing |
| 1.8 km | fourth stream crossing |
| 1.9 km | fifth stream crossing |
| 2.3 km | sixth stream crossing |
| 2.7 km | seventh stream crossing |
| 3.4 km | eighth stream crossing |
| 4.9 km | fork |
| 6.0 km | end of road |
| 6.9 km | spelunkers' campsite |
| 7.8 km | top of the notch |
| 8.0 km | the Promised Land |
| 16.0 km | return to trailhead |

*View from the campsites of unnamed ridges.*

rest is advisable, as the remainder of the tramp offers steep elevation gain in a very short distance.

The path leading to the Promised Land can be found straight ahead through the alders. Leaving the bushes behind, the path skirts a talus slope, then climbs up another talus slope into spruce forest. En route, a window in the Flatheads can be seen behind and to the right.

As you climb through open spruce forest, panoramic views of the Ptolemy Creek valley can be enjoyed until the path swings to the right and climbs up through a small notch. A short reprieve in the steep climb is offered when the trail crosses a small rocky clearing. Above, at the top of a knoll, the path almost flattens and just beyond here, at the edge of the treeline, are campsites used by climbers and spelunkers. If you are backpacking, this is where you will camp.

Towering above are the peaks of Mount Ptolemy. The walls of its soaring rock ridges protect snowfields in niches, even in late summer. Karst formations, frost pockets and false caves dot the whole area. Cleft Cave can be seen above and to the left. Make no mistake, a lot of time can be spent exploring the Alberta side of the ridge.

Nonetheless, the Promised Land beckons. A notch, located due east between Mount Ptolemy and an unnamed mountain southwest of Andy Good Peak, lies straight ahead. At this point, the trail becomes somewhat ill-defined. A trail to the left through the scree appears to lead to a rocky dead end, but instead it offers a high road to the notch. Other trails leading up through the talus also can be found. The notch itself is approximately 40 m wide, lying astride the Continental Divide. The Promised Land is just below on the other side.

The Promised Land is a plateau located approx–imately 150 m below the notch. A trail through the talus leads to the left and eventually down through the rocks to the floor of the plateau. Wandering through this wracked and tortured landscape reveals numerous cavernous openings. While no attempt should be made to access any of these caves (it is highly dangerous without proper equipment and knowledge), nevertheless, no one can resist poking around or trotting over to the southeast edge of the plateau to look down into the valley of Andy Good Creek in British Columbia. Don't be surprised to find you are sharing the plateau with spelunkers. With descriptive names such as Cleft, Ice Hall, Yorkshore Pot and Gargantua, the Promised Land has been a Mecca for experienced spelunkers ever since their discovery in 1969.

If you have chosen to backpack to the campsite, another day can easily be spent exploring the area. For others, it is time to return to the trailhead.

*The notch leading between Mount Ptolemy and Andy Good Peak.*

# 29 TRAIL OF THE SEVEN BRIDGES

If you love high alpine meadows try this hike to the headwaters of Ptolemy Creek at a small jewel-like lake in the heart of the Flathead Range.

From the trailhead, follow the four-wheel-drive road that parallels Ptolemy Creek as it leads back into the Flatheads. The road follows a relatively straight course but is forced to cross the serpentine waters of Ptolemy Creek nine times before it breaks out of the mixed forest into the subalpine region. Because the creek can be high in the spring and has a strong current, kindly souls have provided a variety of bridges that range from mere logs thrown across the creek to more substantial structures. A short distance past the first stream crossing there is a fork. Continue straight ahead, or to the left.

The road gains little elevation until after the seventh stream crossing and it is here that the Flathead Range, consisting of Mount Ptolemy, Andy Good Peak and Mount Parrish, comes into full view. Nearly 1 km later, the road heads down a steep hill to the eighth stream crossing, which has no bridge. Early in the season take care in crossing for the current is strong and the water cold. Once across, climb steadily upward through open pine forest bordered by alder. At a major fork in the road 4.9 km from the trailhead, bear to the left.

The road drops sharply to Ptolemy Creek. Again, there is no bridge, but unless there has been a heavy snow pack from the previous winter, the crossing should present no problem. Waterfalls farther up the valley encourage your ascent toward Andy Good Peak. You next cross an avalanche path where large trees have been snapped by the force of the slides. To the right is a window near the summit of the cliff-faced ridge separating the two forks of Ptolemy Creek.

After the road ends, continue into a high alpine valley that has a tiny emerald lake fed by meltwaters from the snows above. Though the valley is closed on three sides by high mountain walls, a faint trail up scree slopes between Andy Good Peak and Mount Parrish beckons the more intrepid hiker to the saddle separating these two mountains.

Return the way you came.

**Duration** day

**Distance** 16 km return

**Level of Difficulty** Substantial elevation gain on hard-packed road.

**Maximum Elevation** 2165 m

**Elevation Gain** 732 m

**Map** Crowsnest 82 G/10

## Access

Drive to the unsigned Chinook Coal road that lies 4.8 km west of the Travel Alberta Information Centre on Highway 3 west of Coleman. Follow the road for 2.9 km to where the hydro line crosses the road. Pull off to the left and park.

| | |
|---|---|
| 0 m | trailhead and first stream crossing |
| 600 m | fork |
| 1.5 km | second stream crossing |
| 1.7 km | third stream crossing |
| 1.8 km | fourth stream crossing |
| 1.9 km | fifth stream crossing |
| 2.3 km | sixth stream crossing |
| 2.7 km | seventh stream crossing |
| 3.4 km | eighth stream crossing |
| 4.9 km | fork |
| 5.1 km | ninth stream crossing |
| 8.0 km | lake |
| 16.0 km | return to trailhead |

# 30 TWO CABIN TRAIL

This hike leads to the base of Chinook Peak. En route it passes the remnants of an old mine probably dating from the 1920s when numerous mining interests tried their luck at locating a major coal seam, hoping it would lead to riches. This trail tells the tale of one such small company that failed.

The old mine road begins behind the parking lot and follows an unnamed creek up its valley all the way to the mine site. Little waterfalls and rapids break the stillness of the forest. There are numerous creek crossings that, if the water is low, should not necessitate footwear other than hiking boots. In places the needle-strewn road becomes a path through a glade-like setting of poplars, pines and wildflowers.

One kilometre past the trailhead there is an intersection with another old road. If you wish to view a pretty waterfall, turn left and hike along this crossroad for 800 m to a stream crossing. Don't cross, but turn downstream and follow a game trail to where the water splashes over sandstone shelf formations. On a warm day this makes a pleasant rest stop. Return to the mine road and turn left.

Shortly after, another old road intersects the main mine road. Continue straight ahead and at nearly 3 km from the trailhead you reach a wide clearing.

**Duration** half day
**Distance** 10 km return
**Level of Difficulty** Easy walk on old roads and trails.
**Maximum Elevation** 1555 m
**Elevation Gain** 183 m
**Map** Crowsnest 82 G/10

## Access

The trailhead is the parking lot at the Travel Alberta Information Centre near Sentinel on Highway 3 west of Coleman.

| | |
|---|---|
| 0 m | Travel Alberta Information Centre |
| 1.0 km | intersection |
| 1.8 km | waterfall |
| 2.6 km | intersection |
| 2.8 km | clearing |
| 3.0 km | prospect |
| 5.0 km | base of Chinook Peak |
| 10.0 km | return |

*Opposite: The Ray Bagley homestead, 1951. Courtesy Provincial Archives of Alberta, Public Affairs Bureau Collection PA 444/8.*

*Ruins of one of the cabins.*

In amongst the salmonberries and long grasses you can find several cellar depressions, some of them quite large, indicating structures once stood on this spot. Ahead, Chinook Peak beckons you onward.

Beyond the meadow the hiking path soon rejoins the old mine road. The first indication of man's presence here is the remains of a trestle that still straddles the stream. Just past this point, you come upon the mine prospect. Little is known of the Mother Crow Coal Company that prospected here between the years 1920 and 1923. The seam was thin—only 1.5 m thick. Whether it was this factor or others that led to the company's quick demise is unknown. A scramble up the dirt pile, which shows only scant evidence of slack indicating mining activity, confirms the small tonnage taken from this site. A log cabin is located at the far end of the rubble and immediately beyond this is the mine opening.

From the prospect, the road angles to the right and climbs steadily upward for 2 km through evergreen forests past the remains of another cabin. The trail then enters a cleared area just below the scree of Chinook Peak. From here two ridge walks are possible for those of you who yearn for further altitude gain and a fine view.

Return the way you came.

## Chinook Peak

This 2591 m-high mountain that dominates your sightlines during most of this hike is named for the warm, dry Pacific wind that either roars through the pass or arrives in the form of a gentle breeze. When the Geological Survey of Canada was mapping the Flatheads in 1960, they found it necessary to name some of the peaks. Local residents told the Survey that they watch the top of this mountain for indications of an approaching chinook.

# 31 CREEKS AND CANYONS

A small canyon, waterfalls and good views of the Flathead Range make this hike through the forest on old roads worth your while. Along the way is evidence of the pass' rich logging history.

From the parking lot, find the old mine road that follows an unnamed creek up its valley and south toward Chinook Peak. The stream has changed course over the years and now runs over the roadbed in a number of places. If the water is low you should not have to wear footwear other than hiking boots.

Located one kilometre past the trailhead is an intersection with another old road. If you wish to view a waterfall, turn left and hike along this crossroad for 800 m to where the road crosses a stream. Do not cross, but turn downstream and follow a game trail to the falls, which is one of the prettiest in the pass. Return to the old mine road.

Shortly beyond the aforementioned junction, keep a sharp eye out for another old road on the left. Accessed by a rocky streambed, this new road immediately swings to the left and climbs in an easterly direction through stands of pine trees. Old tree stumps nearly hidden in the forest are indicators that this area was once heavily logged. Cross a rather swampy clearing and within 500 m cross a second clearing. An old log cabin with saddle-notched corners lies forgotten on the right through the trees. The trail through the clearing is rather hard to discern, but as it enters the pine forest it once again becomes a distinct roadbed, climbing modestly through another clearing with good views of Chinook Peak.

Shortly beyond this third clearing the road begins to descend. At a fourth clearing the road joins a cutline at Star Creek and begins to descend Star Creek valley. Two kilometres later at an intersection keep to the left, or straight ahead. Stay right at a second fork. Approximately 500 m later there are several intersections within a distance of 100 m. Keep right at the first two and left at the third. Shortly beyond here is a Texas gate.

**Duration** half day

**Distance** 9.4 km

**Level of Difficulty** Easy walk on old roads.

**Maximum Elevation** 1676 m

**Elevation Gain** 122 m

**Map** Crowsnest 82 G/10

## Access

This hike requires two vehicles. Park one vehicle at Star Creek falls trailhead. From Highway 3 take the Coleman Town Centre access into Coleman along 77 St. as far as 18 Ave. Turn right and follow the avenue as it winds around a bluff to 17 Ave. Turn left onto 17 Ave. and continue to 68 St. Turn left and cross the railway tracks. Turn right onto 16 Ave. and drive west for 1.7 km to 54 St. Turn left and follow the rough road up over a small ridge down to Star Creek at a pipeline right-of-way.

Park your second vehicle at the Travel Alberta Information Centre near Sentinel on Highway 3 west of Coleman. The trailhead begins behind the parking lot.

| | |
|---|---|
| 0 m | Travel Alberta Information Centre |
| 1.0 km | intersection |
| 1.8 km | waterfalls |
| 2.6 km | old road |
| 3.2 km | first clearing |
| 3.6 km | second clearing |
| 4.0 km | third clearing |
| 4.9 km | fourth clearing |
| 5.1 km | first intersection |
| 6.8 km | second intersection |
| 7.7 km | third intersection |
| 8.0 km | Texas gate |
| 8.4 km | intersection |
| 8.9 km | three intersections |
| 9.0 km | intersection |
| 9.4 km | Star Creek falls parking |

*Chinook Peak from the trail.*

A great view of the Flathead Range is the backdrop for the small canyon and waterfalls on your right. It is here the road leaves the cutline and the boundary of the forest reserve. At the next fork in the road, bear left. As you descend toward Star Creek falls you come to a series of intersections all within a short distance of each other. Keep right at the first and second intersections, left at a third and right at a fourth. At a final intersection continue straight ahead and downhill to the pipeline right-of-way and the parking area for the Star Creek falls hike.

If you wish to view lower Star Creek falls, turn right off the pipeline at Star Creek and follow an old road nearest the creek that quickly turns into a pathway. To access views of the upper falls see "Star Creek falls" hike on page 112.

## Flathead Range

Named for their deliberately flattened foreheads, the Flathead Indians today are found only in western Montana in the lower Flathead River basin. But sometime prior to 1800 the Flatheads had made their traditional home along the eastern slopes of the Rocky Mountains hunting buffalo all the way from present-day southern Alberta southward to Marias Pass, located just south of Glacier Park. Their territory shrunk considerably when, in 1855, they surrendered this claim in favour of a homeland based in the Bitterroot Valley. However, within 25 years the American government reassigned the tribes to the Flathead Reservation where they remain today.

The Flatheads are also known in historical literature as the Salish. The Salish family of languages is spoken by many of the tribes of the Pacific Northwest.

# 32 STAR CREEK FALLS

Of the several short walks offered in this book, this hike has to be rated near the top of anyone's list. The view of the upper waterfall is spectacular.

Cut across the pipeline right-of-way to the old road nearest the creek and follow it upstream. It quickly becomes a walking path that meanders along a lush canyon whose cliffs are covered with soft mosses. Keep a sharp eye out for venus slippers, the most common of the orchids found in the Rocky Mountains. They bloom relatively early in the season. The path ends at a pretty waterfall tumbling down a chute from the canyon above.

To view the canyon and the more spectacular upper fall, scramble up the mossy hillside to the right before you come to the lower waterfall. A very vague trail leads diagonally to the left and thence to a good trail running along a rocky promontory with overlooks. Below you, Star Creek races through the upper canyon to drop 25 m in its rush to the Crowsnest River. In spring and early summer, the run-off from the Flathead mountains makes this a sight to behold.

From the promontory, follow the good trail back to a fork. Bear left and descend the bank to Star Creek above the fall. Once across the creek, choose the path that leads up the hillsides and doubles back to the top of the canyon. Good views of the canyon, waterfall and the Flathead Range are visible from all along the canyon top. Delightful forget-me-nots, old man's whiskers and violets are sprinkled liberally throughout the grassy slope between Douglas fir trees. A short distance later the path forks temporarily. The path to the left offers a more pleasant walk and after merging with the right-hand braid, brings you out to the pipeline cut. Turn left and descend to Star Creek and your vehicle on the opposite bank.

**Duration** 1 hour

**Distance** 1.6 km return

**Level of Difficulty** Easy walk on trails.

**Maximum Elevation** 1402 m

**Elevation Gain** 62 m

**Map** Crowsnest 82 G/10

## Access

From Highway 3 take the Coleman Town Centre access into Coleman along 77 St. as far as 18 Ave. Turn right and follow the avenue as it winds around a bluff to 17 Ave. Turn left onto 17 Ave. and continue to 68 St. Turn left and cross the railway tracks. Turn right onto 16 Ave. and drive west for 1.7 km to 54 St. Turn left and follow the rough road up over a small ridge down to Star Creek at a pipeline right-of-way.

| | |
|---|---|
| 0 m | trailhead |
| 300 m | waterfall |
| 500 m | first fork via promontory |
| 700 m | creek crossing |
| 1.0 km | second fork |
| 1.6 km | return to trailhead |

Star Creek falls.

# 33 IRONSTONE LOOKOUT

Fire lookout towers make natural destination points for hikers. Not only are there 360 degree panoramas, but a visit to these installations brings an appreciation for the people who occupy these lonely sites. The pull up to the top of the Willoughby Ridge is fairly steep with little shade, so on sunny, hot days take plenty of water.

**Duration** day
**Distance** 10.4 km return
**Level of Difficulty** Fairly steep climb on hard-packed road.
**Maximum Elevation** 2043 m
**Elevation Gain** 579 m
**Map** Crowsnest 82 G/10

## Access

From Highway 3 take the Coleman Town Centre access into town along 77 St. as far as 18 Ave. Here, turn left and go as far as 79 St. Turn right and drive one block to 17 Ave. Turn left for one block and then turn right on 80 St. and follow it to a junction. Turn right onto 81 St. and cross the railway tracks. Turn left onto 13 Ave. and continue to 81 St. Turn right again and follow the street as it curves around a bluff.

From the trailhead, walk along the old road for approximately 50 m to where it crosses York Creek, then bushwhack a short distance upstream to a log bridge. If you haven't done so before leaving town, fill your canteen here as this is your last chance. Regaining the road on the other bank, continue as far as the first fork.

At the fork, bear left uphill, leaving the cooling waters of the stream far behind. The forest soon opens up, allowing views of York Creek valley. At a second fork turn right, then left at a third fork to continue along the main road. At the fourth fork keep to the left. A gate across the road marks the beginning of the long climb to the fire lookout station.

*View of the Flatheads from the trail.*

## Fire Lookouts

Mountain lookouts and fire towers across the province form the first line of defence against forest fires. The work carried out at the lookouts and towers is known as "fixed" detection; this remains the backbone of the detection system of the Alberta Forest Service (AFS). For areas not covered by lookouts and towers, fire detection relies on regular aircraft patrols. Of the 135 towers and lookouts in the province, 25 are mountain lookouts such as the Ironstone Lookout. Each has a working radius of approximately 40 km with some "slopover" into another lookout's area so that fires can be pinpointed more accurately.

In response to a 1953 brief entitled "Forest Fire Protection in Alberta," or simply "The Fire Brief," the AFS was reorganized and expanded to better detect and control fires in the Green Zone, which covers 65 per cent of Alberta. One of the 22 recommendations in "The Fire Brief" was to build more mountain fire lookouts. Ironstone Lookout was built in 1966 and is one of five lookouts presently keeping watch over the Crowsnest Forest Reserve. Owing to the diligent work of the lookout personnel, the Crowsnest Pass is possibly greener now than it has ever been with the result that wildlife, once scarce, now abounds in the pass.

## A Lonely Life

Most lookouts are remote. As you can imagine, it takes a special kind of person to be on a lookout. Needless to say, a critical criterion for the job is sharp eyesight! But equally important is the ability to live alone for long periods of time. A brief chat with the truck driver who drives up Willoughby Ridge once a week with mail and groceries is often the only human contact these people have in the four to six months they are at these isolated vigils. To occupy the time, some paint, make crafts, read or write. Usually at the end of a season, they are quite happy to leave, uncertain whether they want to return. But just as commonly, when the AFS sends out letters of application in midwinter for the next season, they are ready to return for another season among the clouds.

The climb is unrelenting as the fire road switchbacks up Willoughby Ridge. As you climb, better and better views of the dramatic Flathead Range come into sight. Swinging your eyes from south to north, the first peak in the far distance is Mount Pengelly, named in 1917 after the wife of A. J. Campbell who served on the Alberta-British Columbia Boundary Commission. Mount McGladrey is the next mountain, followed by four peaks close together. The first is Mount Coulthard, then comes Andy Good Peak tucked between Mounts Coulthard and Parrish. Senator McLaren, whose lumber mill and saw camps dominated logging on the Alberta side of the Crowsnest Pass, is commemorated by the peak closest to you, while behind McLaren is Mount Parrish named after local pioneer Sherman Parrish.

After a long pull to the top of this 1686 m-high ridge, the hiker is rewarded with a magnificent 360 degree panoramic view from the fire lookout. Lookout personnel lead a lonely life and usually appreciate company; a pleasant visit is almost guaranteed. Often, if asked, they will show you around the lookout. Remember to ask to sign the guest book before you return the way you came.

Where the pavement ends, 81 St. turns into York Creek road. Drive south for approximately 4.5 km. Just before crossing the bridge over York Creek pull over onto an old logging road that joins from the right. This is your trailhead.

| | |
|---|---|
| 0 m | trailhead on logging road |
| 50 m | bridge |
| 600 m | first fork |
| 1.0 km | second fork |
| 1.5 km | third fork |
| 1.7 km | fourth fork |
| 5.2 km | forestry lookout |
| 10.4 km | return to trailhead |

# 34 COULTHARD MOUNTAIN MEADOWS

The Flathead Range offers high alpine meadows, cirques and stupendous views. This particular hike leads along an old road as far as the meadows at the base of Mount Coulthard. Further exploration of the meadows and a steep scramble will be rewarded with views of a tarn, the headwaters of York Creek.

From the trailhead, walk along the old road for approximately 50 m to where it crosses York Creek, then bushwhack a short distance upstream to a log bridge. Regaining the road on the other bank, continue as far as the first fork. Here, bear left. The rough road begins to rise past this point leaving York Creek behind. Soon the forest opens to allow views of the York Creek valley. At a second fork, turn right, then left at a third fork. At a fourth fork with the fire road to Ironstone Lookout bear right to continue along the main road as it heads toward Mount Coulthard. The road climbs steadily through pine and spruce forest and is lined with salmonberries and raspberries in late summer and early autumn. At yet a fifth fork, keep to the right and cross York Creek. A good bridge built for snowmobilers makes the creek crossing easy.

**Duration** day
**Distance** 11.6 km return
**Level of Difficulty** Moderate elevation gain on hard-packed road.
**Maximum Elevation** 1981 m
**Elevation Gain** 549 m
**Map** Crowsnest 82 G/10

## Access

From Highway 3 take the Coleman Town Centre access into town along 77 St. as far as 18 Ave. Here, turn left and go as far as 79 St. Turn right and drive one block to 17 Ave. Turn left for one block and then turn right on 80 St. and follow it to a junction. Turn right onto 81 St. and cross the railway tracks. Turn left onto 13 Ave. and continue to 81 St. Turn right again and follow the street as it curves around a bluff. Where the pavement ends, 81 St. turns into York Creek road. Drive south for approximately 4.5 km. Just before crossing the bridge over York Creek, pull over onto an old logging road that joins from the right. This is your trailhead.

| | |
|---|---|
| 0 m | trailhead on logging road |
| 50 m | bridge |
| 600 m | fork |
| 1.0 km | second fork |
| 1.5 km | third fork |
| 1.7 km | fourth fork |
| 3.4 km | fifth fork |
| 3.5 km | bridge |
| 5.5 km | cabin remains |
| 5.8 km | end of track by stream |
| 11.6 km | return to trailhead |

*Waterfall on York Creek. The creek was named by early British settlers and miners after the cathedral town of York in England.*

*Pit at York Creek.*

The road now climbs relentlessly through forest for 2 km with the high rock peak of Mount Coulthard drawing you like a magnet. As the road breaks out of the thick forest, remains of an old cabin appear on your right. Just beyond this point the road disintegrates into a grassy swath continuing through trees as far as a small stream that is the infant York Creek. From here, enticing meadows lead up to the right of Mount Coulthard to a saddle on the north–east ridge. In front of you a mountain tarn is found above and behind the rocky promontory, a visit neces–sitating a very steep bushwhack through shrubbery.

Return the way you came.

Once back at the trailhead, cross the bridge over York Creek and climb down the banks to the creek below. In late summer, the area is overgrown with long grass and low shrubs, but by poking around you can find evidence of a 1913 mine site belonging to International Coal & Coke Company of Coleman. Concrete foundations of a hoist house, fan house and other buildings are located on both sides of the creek. To view a beautiful waterfall, walk farther downstream. Flat rocks make an ideal seat while soaking your tired feet in the icy waters.

## Mount Coulthard

Named by local residents after a mining engineer and the general manager of the West Canadian Coal Company in 1910, this 2642 m-high mountain is one of the better-known peaks in the Flatheads. For it is here that a large cave can be found, although the entrance is actually on the other side of the mountain above North York Creek.

# 35 NORTH YORK CIRQUE

An airplane crash site still strewn with wreckage adds a sobering note to an otherwise upbeat hike. Starting near the International Coal & Coke site on York Creek, this hike begins by rising gently alongside both York and North York creeks, but once past the final bridge, climbs much more sharply to the crash site. You can continue into a high alpine cirque.

From the trailhead walk along the old road for approximately 50 m to where it crosses York Creek, then bushwhack upstream a short distance to a log bridge. Regain the road on the other bank and continue as far as the first junction. Here, bear to the right. Within a short distance there is another

*Waterfall above the crash site looking toward the cirque.*

**Duration** day

**Distance** 13.3 km return

**Level of Difficulty** Significant elevation gain on hard-packed road.

**Maximum Elevation** 2256 m

**Elevation Gain** 793 m

**Map** Crowsnest 82 G/10

## Access

From Highway 3 take the Coleman Town Centre access into town along 77 St. as far as 18 Ave. Here, turn left and go as far as 79 St. Turn right and drive one block to 17 Ave. Turn left for one block and then turn right on 80 St. and follow it to a junction. Turn right onto 81 St. and cross the railway tracks. Turn left onto 13 Ave. and continue to 81 St. Turn right again and follow the street as it curves around a bluff. Where the pavement ends 81 St. turns into York Creek road. Drive south for approximately 4.5 km. Just before crossing the bridge over York Creek, pull over onto an old logging road that joins from the right. This is your trailhead.

| | |
|---|---|
| 0 m | trailhead |
| 50 m | bridge |
| 600 m | first junction |
| 900 m | bridge |
| 1.2 km | second junction |
| 2.3 km | third junction |
| 3.7 km | fourth junction |
| 4.4 km | caves |
| 6.0 km | North York Creek crossing |
| 6.3 km | crash site |
| 6.7 km | cirque |
| 13.3 km | return to trailhead |

# The Aeroplane Crash

It was January 9, 1946, when a Royal Canadian Air Force Dakota was reported missing en route from Cranbrook, British Columbia to Winnipeg. Several days passed before local forestry officials, Harry Boulton, Bill Ludlow and Jim McGilligett, found the wreckage. It appeared the seven servicemen were killed instantly when the DC-3 smashed into one of the peaks and tumbled into this valley. Because of the heavy snowfall and fallen timber, it took rescue crews 10 days to reach and bring out the badly charred bodies on toboggans.

This was not the only fatal air crash to have occurred in the Crowsnest Pass. A year later, on March 15, 1947, a converted Arson aircraft owned by the contracting firm, Fred Mannix and Company Ltd. of Calgary, was en route to Michel, British Columbia where Mannix was involved in coal stripping operations. While attempting to land at an emergency landing field between Sentinel and Coleman, the aircraft hit a tree and smashed into the riverbank killing all four executives on board.

*Tail section of the crashed DC-3.*

*Dakota DC-3 over the Rocky Mountains. Courtesy Department of National Defense IWC 89-63.*

stream crossing, but this time there is a substantial bridge built to facilitate snowmobile traffic in the winter. Climb up a hill. Halfway up the steep grade turn right at a junction onto a shortcut. On the top of the rise, continue along the roadway through pine forest, which in early summer is underlain with salmonberries, Indian paintbrushes and silky lupines. At a third junction bear to the right once again. It will be approximately 1.5 km before you arrive at a fourth junction. Ignore the bridge that crosses North York Creek. Instead, swing to the right, climbing steeply uphill.

Soon the road breaks out of the forest into alpine terrain with views of Mount Coulthard, Mount Parrish and Andy Good Peak. When opposite Mount McLaren, the many caves for which this area is renowned become evident. The action of slightly acidic water and also glaciation account for the massive network of underground and above ground channels that cover this area. Several shallow caves can be easily reached by a short bushwhack up McLaren's slopes, but none leads to a channel network. In fact, most channels in the caves are too small to access.

Under the watchful eye of the mammoth entrance to Coulthard Cave above and to your left, you cross North York Creek yet once again. No bridge is required. From here, the road continues sharply uphill to the remains of an airplane, which you can find just off to your left. Dating from 1946, wreckage of the DC-3 is still strewn amongst this beautiful high alpine country. Meadows of fireweed, purple asters and wild chives grow in great abundance close to the remnants of a wing section. The road ends here so linger awhile below the upper reach of North York Creek as it spills down through snowfields from the cirque above.

To access the cirque between Mount Coulthard and Andy Good Peak, cross the creek and locate the trail leading up beside the stream into high alpine meadows. Even in late summer, the meadows are a delight, covered as they are with dainty forget-me-nots and lacy cow parsnip. Once in the cirque you come to a small tarn, or lake, the headwaters of North York Creek.

Return the way you came.

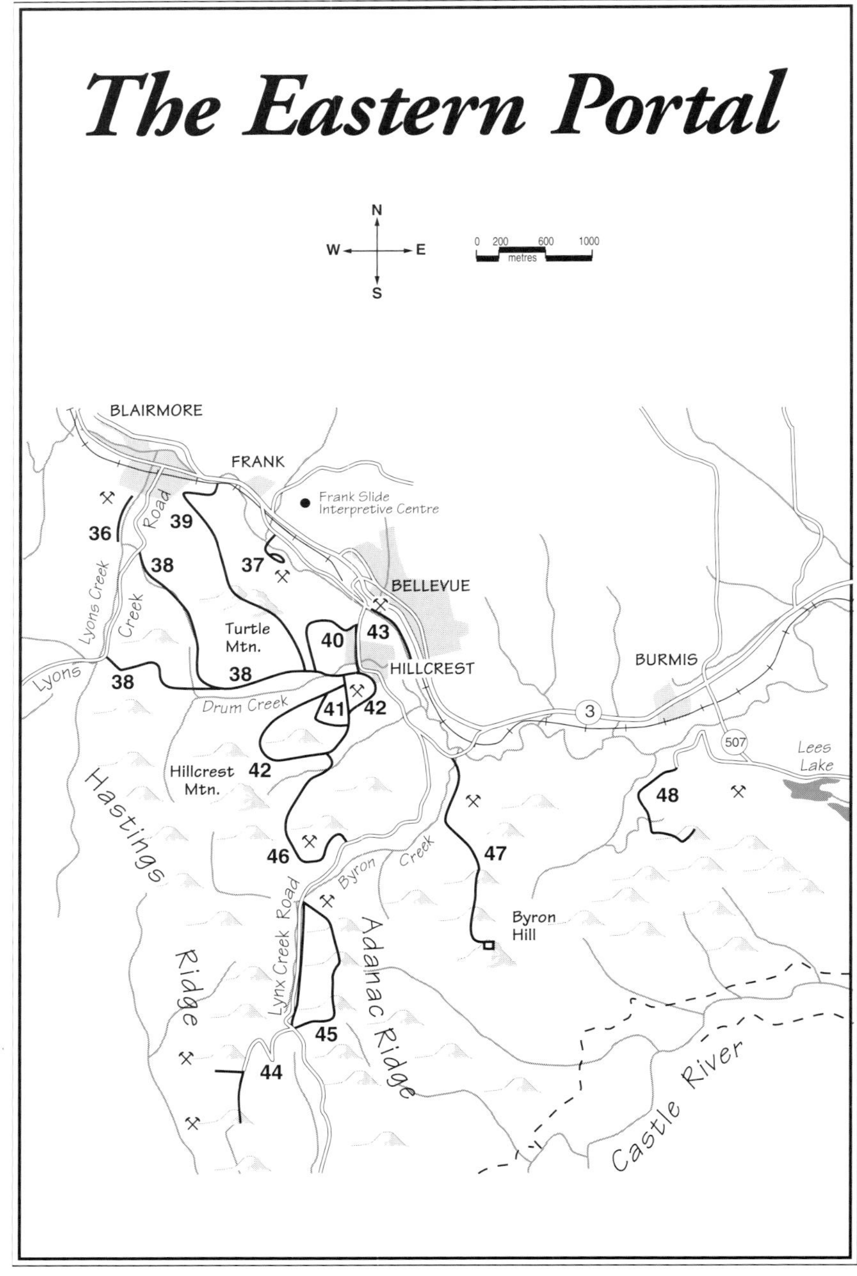
The Eastern Portal
N
W
E
S
0 200 600 1000
metres
BLAIRMORE
FRANK
Frank Slide
Interpretive Centre
BELLEVUE
HILLCREST
BURMIS
36
39
38
37
Turtle
Mtn.
40
43
38
38
41
42
Hillcrest
Mtn.
42
46
47
48
45
44
Lyons Creek
Creek
Road
Lyons
Drum Creek
Hastings
Ridge
Lynx Creek Road
Byron
Creek
Adanac Ridge
Byron
Hill
3
507
Lees
Lake
Castle River

# Blairmore

**Previous Names** Tenth Siding, Nitay-stato-ksisokyopi, The Springs

The railway siding that was created here when the Canadian Pacific Railway built its Crowsnest line in 1897-98 was number ten, hence the first name given to this location, Tenth Siding. Tenth Siding was also known locally as The Springs since the hamlet was the closest locality to the sulphur springs and spa located at the western foot of Turtle Mountain. (See "Turtle Mountain" hike.) The Blackfoot also had a name for the general area near present-day Blairmore. When Senator McLaren relocated his sawmill west of the village, the Blackfoot named this part of the pass Nitay-stato-ksisokyopi, which means "where they rip logs."

There are two possible origins for the current name of Blairmore. One version claims the town was renamed Blairmore after A. G. Blair (1844-1907), the minister of railways in the Laurier government. The other story has the town named after a Mr. Blair and a Mr. More, both railway contractors who built this portion of the line through the pass. The town was officially named Blairmore on September 15, 1898, the day the rail line was completed to the hamlet.

Blairmore is the hub of the Municipality of Crowsnest Pass. The largest of the old pass towns, Blairmore serves as the main shopping and service centre. It is also home to the Gushul Photo Studio. Thomas Gushul and his wife Lena were well-known photographers in the pass for 50 years beginning in 1914. Years of work resulted in tens of thousands of photographs, many portraitures but also photographs of the mines, towns and events. The photographs are now housed at the Glenbow Archives in Calgary.

Blairmore's beginnings were modest. Upon completion of the Canadian Pacific Railway line through the Crowsnest Pass in 1899, a hamlet appeared at this railway siding. Indeed, it was Harry Lyon, the second station agent at the time, who first took advantage of the location to build a log store to serve the miners at the Frank mine. Within a few years, the village boasted three hotels and several businesses despite the fact it had no mine. That changed in 1901 when, shortly after the incorporation of Blairmore as a village, West Canadian Collieries purchased property near the siding from a third party. Combined with

*The town of Blairmore.*

*Today the Gushul Studio has been renovated by the Alberta Historical Resources Foundation and is used by the University of Lethbridge as a studio for artists-in-residence.*

its holdings at Bellevue and Lille, West Canadian Collieries now owned 4,858 hectares, making it the second largest landholder in the pass next to the Leitch Collieries. When, in April 1909, the company announced it had struck a major seam south of town, the future of the village was assured. Housing prices skyrocketed from $600 a lot to $1,500. Within a matter of months, 15 new homes, a drug store, a barber shop, a hardware store and a law office sprang up. Blairmore expanded dramatically after West Canadian Collieries' Greenhill mine opened north of Blairmore in 1913. The company, short of office space, contracted the construction of new offices west of the original townsite. The so-called New Townsite stretches between 127 Street and 123 Street and boasts of such buildings as the company's general office, the Greenhill Hotel, the Greenhill apartments and the Collieries' duplex located on 21 Avenue.

Complete reliance on the mining industry meant a local economy entirely subject to the vicissitude of the coal market. In the early years of the 20th century, there were a number of attempts to diversify by such companies as the Rocky Mountain Cement Company, which was established here in 1907. With local limestone deposits being as much as 95 per cent pure, it appeared as though the cement plant could only be a success. Indeed, in 1910 production reached 6,000 barrels of cement, which was sold to markets as far away as Spokane in the state of Washington. In 1914, the records show that 90 men were employed in the plant. The slowing of the economy because of the First World War, though, forced the plant to close in August of the same year.

Certainly, coal mining in the pass was a volatile occupation. Strikes for better wages and conditions marked the early years, the most violent occurring in 1932 when the coal companies threatened to cut wages. Once again the miners and management squared off. A huge demonstration on 1 May centred around the gazebo on the main street. Four days later the R.C.M.P., responding to management fears of "communists" and agitators, rode through the crowd swinging their truncheons. Management fears of the labouring class were somewhat justified. Several months earlier, miner sympathizers swept the ballot box in local elections. The new town council immediately declared 1 May a holiday and renamed the main street Tim Buck Boulevard, after the jailed Communist Party of Canada leader.

Since the closure of the Greenhill mine in 1958, Blairmore has concentrated on service sector industries.

# 36 LYONS CREEK RAVINE

Whether a relaxing evening walk or an afternoon outing complete with picnic basket, this trail is a charmer. The babbling Lyons Creek, picnic sites and a heart-shaped pool at the base of a waterfall will delight the whole family.

**Duration** 2 hours
**Distance** 2.6 km return
**Level of Difficulty** Informal trail, stream crossings.
**Maximum Elevation** 1372 m
**Elevation Gain** 30 m
**Map** Blairmore 82 G/9

## Access

From Highway 3 take the Blairmore Centre access (129 St.) into town. Cross the railway tracks and proceed to 19 Ave. Turn left and continue over the bridge as far as 132 St. Turn right. Turn right again on 16 Ave. Go past an old garage and continue uphill. Shortly after the pavement ends there is a fork. Keep right and go 150 m to a pipeline right-of-way. Park here.

| | |
|---|---|
| 0 m | cut line |
| 300 m | northerly end of S. Blairmore mine |
| 1.0 km | waterfall |
| 2.6 km | return to trailhead |

From your parked vehicle, walk in a westerly direction and pass through the fence. Follow the ATV track as it leads you along the pipeline right-of-way down to Lyons Creek. Turn left. A fence appears to block your way into the ravine, but an opening has been left that allows you to access the path on the other side. Prior to 1995 there were a number of paths on this lower portion of the hike, and here and there picnic tables complete with

*The heart-shaped pool.*

## South Blairmore Mine

When you walk from the trailhead along the pipeline right-of-way to go to Lyons Creek, to your right just beyond the trees and below was the site of West Canadian Collieries' South Blairmore mine. Today, little remains of the mine site, the last of the coal slack piles having been removed recently. But between 1909 and 1914 the South Blairmore mine exploited a 3.7 m-thick seam of excellent quality coal. December 1909 saw the mine producing 300 tonnes daily. Three years later, the main gangway had progressed 1676 m and a wooden tipple, a wash house, lamp house, power house, weigh scale, a horse stable and a spur line to the Canadian Pacific Railway had been built. An electrical generating plant housed in the boiler building provided electricity for the town of Blairmore for many years. Nearly 500,000 tons of coal were extracted from the South Blairmore mine before irregularities in the seams forced its closure in 1914 in favour of West Canadian's new Greenhill mine north of Blairmore.

*South Blairmore mine, 1913. Courtesy Glenbow Archives, NA 3903-30.*

campfire pits could be found. The spring flood of 1995 undercut the streambed, toppling large trees that now obliterate the original path. However, not all is lost. Local residents have been determined to continue to use this picturesque spot and flag markers now outline your route. You cross and recross the stream a number of times, but the numerous rocks in the streambed make for dry crossings. As you progress up the creek, interesting cliff faces appear, first on one side and then on the other. A lovely waterfall, spraying over smooth rock formations, and a naturally formed heart-shaped pool at its base make a fitting conclusion to this relaxing walk. While the pool may beckon on a warm day, its temperature may shock you for it is fed from the meltwaters of Willoughby Ridge.

Return the way you came.

## Frank

*Frank after the slide, ca. 1911. Courtesy Provincial Archives of Alberta, Archives Collection A 1770.*

When driving through the Crowsnest Pass you can zip by Frank without realizing it as the hamlet is unsigned on the highway. But wait. A large restaurant and art gallery indicate that this cluster of homes is, perhaps, of some significance. And indeed it is! For it was close to here that the first coal mine in the Crowsnest Pass opened in 1901.

In that year, Sam Gebo and Henry L. Frank, both Americans with mining experience, gave $30,000 to Henry Pelletier to obtain the rights to mine coal at the base of Turtle Mountain. The townsite, named after Mr. Frank, was located close to the mine on a flat of land currently occupied by a few businesses. By September, Frank and Gebo were ready to host a celebration to mark the opening of their Canadian-American Coal and Coke Company. The two entrepreneurs went all out to launch their enterprise. A French chef was hired to put on a luncheon for nearly 3,000 invited guests who had been transported to the townsite by the Canadian Pacific Railway at special low rates for the occasion. The new hotel, "bedecked with bunting," hosted a ball all afternoon and into the evening. Lacrosse, races, and other field events were held on the field close to the river. Although no cash prizes were given, medals worth more than $500 were awarded to the winners. To impress on their guests the potential of the mine, the owners ran excursions to the mine in coal cars covered with clean, white canvas. The 24 miners' cottages, "neatly painted, each removed 50 feet from its nearest neighbour, radiated a look of prosperity and permanency." A month later, businessmen began opening their stores on what became Dominion Avenue, and within a year, a local newspaper editor waxed that "what was one year ago the haunt of the deer, where the howl of the coyote was heard nightly, is now a hive of industry, furnishing home and employment for hundreds of families." Frank could boast a population of 600 people.

The initial success of the mine and town was placed in jeopardy in the wee hours of April 29, 1903, when, without any warning, some 30 million cubic metres of limestone broke off from the face of Turtle Mountain. Within seconds, part of the town of Frank was buried under the rubble, costing approximately 70 people their lives. In the aftermath of the slide, the townsite was relocated to its present location, north of the highway, owing to continuing concerns about the likelihood of another rock slide. Surprisingly, the slide did not close down the mine and within a month it was business as usual. The company made improvements to the surface plant and built the Rocky Mountain Sanatorium adjacent to a nearby cold sulphur spring. The mine and sanatorium continued to operate until 1918, when they closed, leaving the town of Frank bereft of sustaining a local economy.

# 37 THE FRANK MINE

This short hike leads you past the old townsite of Frank and across the Crowsnest River to the base of Turtle Mountain and the remains of the Frank mine.

At the trailhead, you will notice two cairns. One was donated by the Blairmore Lions Club in memory of the 70-odd people who lost their lives in the rock avalanche on April 29, 1903. The other is the headstone of Delbert Ennis (1895-1975) and his sister Gladys (Ennis) Verquin (1902-1993). Both children miraculously escaped death when a chunk of Turtle Mountain crashed down upon an unsuspecting, sleeping town. The rest of their family were not so fortunate; they are buried under

*The cairns at the beginning of the trail.*

**Duration** 2 hours
**Distance** 1.2 km return
**Level of Difficulty** Easy path; river crossing followed by some bushwhacking.
**Maximum Elevation** 1280 m
**Elevation Gain** negligible
**Map** Blairmore 82 G/9

## Access

Turn off Highway 3 at the West Hillcrest access. Just after crossing the railway tracks, turn right onto a hard surfaced road. Three and one-half kilometres later, at the west end of the Frank Slide, there is a small turnout on the right. Park here.

| | |
|---|---|
| 0 m | trailhead |
| 100 m | gravel track |
| 400 m | Crowsnest River |
| 600 m | Frank mine |
| 1.2 km | return to trailhead |

# The Frank Mine

In early 1901, Sam Gebo and Henry L. Frank obtained the rights to mine coal at the base of Turtle Mountain. By September, the Canadian-American Coal and Coke Company became the first mine to open in the Crowsnest Pass. By pushing forward 18 m a day, the company had a main tunnel 1371 m long by October 1902. Above ground work proceeded as rapidly, with the surface plant and the spur line from the mine to the Canadian Pacific main line being ready for use by the end of 1901. An incredible 15,000 tonnes were taken from the mountain in the first year of operation and by the end of 1902, the mine had produced more than 175,000 tonnes.

This auspicious beginning was threatened on that fateful day at the end of April 1903. Huge slabs of limestone crashed down on the sleepy town and in a matter of seconds the east end of Frank and the entire surface plant were destroyed. Inside the mine was the night shift—trapped! Although not understanding what had happened, the 19 miners knew something was wrong when coal broke away from the coal face and rock fell from the roof. One entrance was blocked with rubble, another was flooded with water. Two men died. The rest then had a choice of digging their way out of the entrance or digging a new tunnel. They chose the latter and emerged 14 hours later to an unbelievable sight. It may seem incredible, but within 30 days the company had the men and boys back in the mine working.

The mine was, by Crowsnest Pass standards, successful. Before it closed in 1918, the company had extracted 1,457,000 tonnes of steam coal. On the other hand, the Frank mine was undoubtedly one of the most dangerous. Its 4 m-wide seam dipped at an angle of 82 degrees! This forced the men to climb rope ladders into their "rooms" where they worked at the coal face. The return journey was fraught with danger as they swung out on the ropes in near darkness. More than one man died when his rope or ladder broke. The pitch also exposed the miners to falling coal and rock, and between 1901 and 1907, seven miners were killed through this cause alone. A particularly nasty job in the Frank mine was that of the "bucker." If the chute plugged with coal, it was the job of the bucker to loosen the pile by climbing into the chute and kicking the coal. By bracing themselves against one of the sides of the chute, the buckers normally performed the job without incident. At the Frank mine, however, at least seven men died by falling down the chutes. Mine inspectors were suspicious Gebo and Frank placed their men at special risk by demanding they withdraw more coal from the pillars that supported the roof than was safe, but Gebo replied by demanding the provincial government allow Canadian-American Coal and Coke Company "to carry on by the same system of operations at the Frank mine" as mining companies did in France and Belgium.

It was neither the high death rate nor the slide that forced the closure of the Frank mine. There does not appear to be a conclusive reason, although an unchecked fire that spread throughout the mine seems to be the most logical answer.

Rebuilding the mine entrance after the Frank Slide, 1903. Photo W. G. Barcley. Courtesy Glenbow Archives, NA 147-36.

the rubble. When Ennis died at age 80, he chose to be buried near where he had lost his family. Nearly 20 years later his sister chose likewise.

A short distance past the cairns turn left onto a gravel track. The field to the right was once occupied by buildings on the eastern outskirts of Frank and if you poke about you can still find cellar depressions here and there. Three hundred metres later, the track becomes a mere path beaten through the tall grass. A short distance later, you arrive at the banks of the Crowsnest River. To reach the remains of the Frank mine, you must cross the river and gain the slack pile on the opposite side. Crossing the river can be a little tricky owing to its fairly strong current and high water levels in spring and early summer. We suggest this hike is best done in late summer when water levels tend to be much lower. Pick your spot carefully as there are deeper channels and holes.

Once across, follow the old slack-covered railbed southeast to the main ventilation shaft of the Frank mine. To find the shaft and the fan, which sucked out the foul air from the mine, scramble through poplar stands and over rock piles. The bushwhack is worth it. The large fan, which is partly obliterated by poplars, dates from the beginning of the mining operation and is, therefore, one of the earliest extant fans to be found in the pass today.

After exploring the area, retrace your steps to the coal slack and recross the river back to your vehicle.

## The Lime Kilns

En route to the trailhead for the Frank Mine hike, on your right at a bend in the road, you passed the remains of the Winnipeg Fuel and Supply Company lime kilns.

Lime is used in the mortar of brick buildings and in cement. At the turn of the 20th century the Canadian prairies were experiencing a building and construction boom as hundreds of thousands of eastern Canadians, Americans and Europeans sought land and work in the west. To supply the much needed lime for the buildings, the Winnipeg Fuel and Supply Company built first two, and then three kilns here, tapping into the limestone rubble of the Frank Slide. The rock was dumped into the kilns where it was baked to the point that it broke down, producing lime. After it had cooled inside the kilns, the lime was drawn from the bottom of the kilns and stored in barrels to await shipment east. A small settlement known as Lime City sprang up adjacent to the kilns where the workers lived.

The building boom peaked and burst just before the outbreak of the First World War in 1914. By the end of the war in 1918, the lack of demand for lime forced the company to close its operations.

*The lime kilns ca. 1913-15. Courtesy Provincial Archives of Alberta, Archives Collection A 1761.*

*The lime kilns in 1999.*

# 38 DRUM CREEK

Beginning at the surface plant of the Hillcrest mine, this hike gives you the satisfaction of looping around the south and west slopes of Turtle Mountain. For those people who like a more challenging hike, there is an option that leads to a truly magnificent viewpoint overlooking the Flathead and High Rock ranges.

Walk up the gravel road. En route to the Hillcrest mine surface plant, bear to the right at four intersections. Just beyond the fourth intersection are the remains of the power house and other buildings related to the Hillcrest Collieries. Keep to the right at yet a fifth fork. The babbling waters and small cataracts of Drum Creek accompany you to a green pump house and a concrete dam. Cross Drum Creek.

**Duration** half day
**Distance** 9 km
**Option** 8 km
**Level of Difficulty** Hard-packed roads and forest trails.
**Maximum Elevation** 1677 m
**Elevation Gain** 396 m
**Option** 366 m
**Elevation Loss** 366 m
**Option** 213 m
**Map** Blairmore 82 G/9

## Access

This hike requires two vehicles. From Highway 3 take the Blairmore Centre access (129 St.) into town. Cross the railway tracks and proceed to 19 Ave. Turn left and continue over the bridge as far as 132 St. Turn right. Turn right again on 16 Ave. Go past an old garage and continue uphill. Shortly after the pavement ends there is a fork. Keep right and go 150 m to a pipeline right-of-way. Park your first vehicle here. If you decide on the option, park your first vehicle 3.6 km down the same road.

For both hikes, take the West Hillcrest access from Highway 3 into Hillcrest along 9 Ave. A few hundred metres past the railway tracks there is a fork. Take the left-hand fork to continue on 9 Ave. to 230 St. Turn right and park near the corner of 230 St. and 7 Ave. Your trailhead is the gravel road leading uphill.

*The trail in Drum Creek above the beaver ponds, looking toward the gap.*

## Common or Field Horsetail

**Scientific Name** *Equisetum arvense*
**Other Name** Scouring-rush

Horsetails can be found in the montane and lower subalpine zones in the Front Ranges. Although they are usually associated with marshy areas, surprisingly, they can live in rather drier conditions. The horsetails seen on this hike, though, grow adjacent to a streambed.

A perennial plant, horsetail has a frilly look owing to its numerous side branches. Common horsetail has two types of shoots. The brownish, fertile ones come up early in spring and are unbranched. The green, sterile shoots are branched and come up later in the season.

The "cones" at the tops of the fertile shoots of horsetails are quite edible if eaten in small quantities; gluttonous consumption of this plant, though, produces symptoms of poisoning owing to the toxins present in the plant! Boil the young fertile heads in place of asparagus, or boil the stems to use as a diuretic just as the Blackfoot did. Today, many herbalists use horsetails for skin treatments because of its high silica content. Because of the high silica content, the green shoots are sometimes used for scouring blackened cookware and other dishes, hence the name scouring-rush. The silica also causes scours in horses that happen to eat horsetails.

*Horsetails. Photo Julie Hrapko.*

| | |
|---|---|
| 0 m | trailhead |
| 70 m | first intersection |
| 300 m | second intersection |
| 400 m | third intersection and water tower |
| 600 m | fourth intersection and surface plant |
| 700 m | fifth intersection |
| 900 m | green pumphouse and concrete dam at Drum Creek |
| 3.6 km | Drum Creek and fork with option |
| 5.6 km | meadow |
| 7.4 km | fork |
| 8.2 km | cutline |
| 9.0 km | Lyons Creek road |

Option

| | |
|---|---|
| 5.1 km | top of the ridge |
| 8.0 km | Lyons Creek road |

Keep left along the main road that eventually leaves the valley bottom and climbs above the creek in a series of short, steep steps. At the top, pause. Below and to the left is a large beaver dam that has flooded parts of the roadway ahead. There are four locations where the road crosses the creek. In high summer, the crossings are not difficult, but in early spring the run-off dictates a search along the streambed for suitable crossings. It is so moist that in places large clumps of horsetails can be seen growing along the edge. After an agreeable jaunt through the gap between Turtle Mountain and Hillcrest Mountain, the road descends to Drum Creek. The option crosses the creek.

For those who do not wish to take the option, do not cross the creek. A small path to the right leads gently upward for 300 m. Once past here, the trail becomes difficult to discern because of deadfall timber. If you are in doubt, climb above the north fork of Drum Creek on your left. En route, there is a series of small meadows. Continue climbing to the top of a pass, the summit of which is hidden in the pine and spruce forest. Now for a long descent. Along the way there are several forks in the path but they all rejoin. Salmonberries and alders lining this forest pathway make this a most pleasant section to hike.

At the bottom of a steep descent, the path forks. Keep to the right. A 500 m walk along a pine cone-strewn path suddenly brings you parallel to a cutline. The path, alternately wide and then narrow, reenters the forest for the final descent to the Lyons Creek road. Your vehicle should be nearby.

**Option**—Ridge: From Drum Creek crossing, the road climbs very steeply in switchbacks to a ridge top, a northerly extension of Hastings Ridge. On a warm day, this can be a very hot tramp, but exhilarating views of the Flathead Range, the High Rock Range and Crowsnest Mountain are a fitting reward for reaching the top.

Rest awhile in the shade of the pines before beginning an equally steep descent. In descending there are good vistas of Willoughby Ridge, named after an early pioneer family in the Crowsnest Pass. The hike ends where the road joins the Lyons Creek road. Turn right and walk back to pick up your first vehicle.

# 39 TURTLE MOUNTAIN

One of the most popular hikes in the Crowsnest Pass with local residents loops up one flank of Turtle Mountain, crosses over the summit ridge with its deep fissures, then descends the other side of the mountain. The views from the top of the north peak are nothing less than spectacular.

From the Shell Station cross Highway 3 and walk west approximately 200 m to a small turnoff. Cross the railway tracks and follow a well-worn path past a couple of old lumber buildings. At a fork, take the left-hand or lower path to the sulphur spring. If the wind is from the east, you will be able to smell the spring long before you actually arrive. Many believe in the curative effects of sulphur water and by the look of the path, it would appear Crowsnest Pass residents still rely on the waters to restore their good health. A pool of milky water at the base of the mountain is what they have come for. The spring is cold, so any thoughts you have had of soaking in a hot sulphur spring are quickly dissipated.

From the spring, continue eastward along the path for approximately 100 m to an ascending cutline on your right. At the top of the cut, turn right onto a rough dirt road and walk almost as far as a chain link fence protecting you from an old limestone quarry. Here, you must scramble up the cliff to access the trail up the mountain, which is at first indistinct, though as you get higher it becomes more obvious. On the lower part of the north ridge, you climb through spruce and pine woods, but soon leave the protection of the trees for a spine of exposed rock that you follow all the way to the top of the north peak. There are several forks along the way, but they all rejoin so it does not matter which path you follow. Yarrow, buttercup, krummholz, low bush cranberry and cinquefoil sprinkle the pathway as long as the Frank Slide Interpretive Centre, the Livingstone Range and Bluff Mountain stay in view.

The final stretch is a long, steep pull overlooking the Frank Slide. Now and again, from cracks in the ridge you can look out over the scar left when the slice of limestone broke away from the northeast face. Your climb up to the north peak is over solid limestone, but in the area of the saddle between

**Duration** full day

**Distance** 7.8 km

**Level of Difficulty** Steep climb on a well-used trail up exposed slopes. Some scree and easy scrambling on descent.

**Maximum Elevation** 2165 m

**Elevation Gain** 915 m

**Elevation Loss** 823 m

**Map** Blairmore 82 G/9

## Access

The traverse of Turtle Mountain requires two vehicles. From the West Hillcrest access on Highway 3, drive your first vehicle into Hillcrest along 9 Ave. Located a few hundred metres past the railway tracks is a fork. Take the left-hand fork and continue on 9 Ave. to 230 St. Turn right and park near the corner of 230 St. and 7 Ave.

Park your second vehicle at the Shell Service Station on Highway 3 between Frank and Blairmore. This is your trailhead.

| | |
|---|---|
| 0 km | trailhead |
| 140 m | turnoff |
| 170 m | sulphur spring |
| 1.0 km | beginning of trail |
| 4.0 km | top of north peak |
| 4.3 km | top of south peak |
| 6.8 km | flume and trestle and Drum Creek crossing |
| 7.1 km | first fork |
| 7.2 km | second fork and surface plant |
| 7.4 km | third fork and water tower |
| 7.5 km | fourth fork |
| 7.7 km | fifth fork |
| 7.8 km | trailhead |

## Monitoring the Mountain

In the immediate aftermath of the slide, there was much fear of another rock avalanche. The man of the hour was William Pearce, territorial mines inspector, who in May 1903 ordered "pickets" to be placed on top of the mountain where they could be seen from below. Any deviation in their position was to indicate another slide was imminent. Later, measurements between markers, called "chaining," were taken periodically to record any widening of the fissures on the top of the mountain. A story is told that a tourist was reassured of the safety of the mountain because it had just been rechained!

*Frank Slide from the summit ridge of Turtle Mountain, August 1951. Courtesy Provincial Archives of Alberta, Public Affairs Bureau Collection PA 172/2.*

## The Rocky Mountain Sanatorium

Sulphur springs have long been known for their curative effects of any number of rheumatoid conditions. The first person to exploit the potential of Turtle Mountain's cold sulphur spring was William Lee, an early cattleman in the district. He erected a log hotel at this location, heating the sulphurous water over outdoor fires and then transporting the hot water to wash tubs inside his hotel for his clients. Then, in 1905, the Canadian-American Coal and Coke Company, which operated the mine at Frank, purchased the site and in 1911 built a large spa north of the railway track. The sulphur waters were piped to a three-storey building called the Rocky Mountain Sanatorium, which boasted steam baths taken in tubs of galvanized iron, a bar and a poolroom in the basement, a French chef, and fresh flowers and champagne for the guests. By 1912, the coal company had built a rustic bridge over the Crowsnest River north of the Sanatorium and had set up a small zoo! Patients in wheelchairs and even on stretchers were taken there to enjoy the sunshine in the lee of Bluff Mountain. The spring was not only popular with patients from outside the pass. The local people "took the waters" as well—a glassful for 10 straight days each spring was recommended!

Sulphur springs, ca. 1911. Courtesy Provincial Archives of Alberta, Archives Collection A 1762.

During the First World War, the Canadian government took over what was by then a floundering business and converted the health spa into a hospital for soldiers suffering from tuberculosis and the effects of mustard gas poisoning. The steam and bath rooms were renovated by installing tubs measuring 3 m long by 1 m wide. When the Central Alberta Sanatorium opened in Calgary in 1922, the Rocky Mountain Sanatorium closed. The building was demolished in 1928.

the two summits the rock is cracked, fissured and rotten. Once across, jaunt along the ridge to the summit of the south peak. Near the edge of the precipice, some energetic soul has planted a pole with a red flag. The path ends in a knife-edge shortly beyond the flagpole.

To reach your second vehicle, descend by heading east onto rough scree below the south ridge. The path is difficult to find at first. If in doubt, aim for the farmstead that lies directly below. The slope is steep at the top and at times requires scrambling over rocky outcroppings. Along the way you should pass two aerial photography targets and red spray paint markings on rock faces. A distinct path appears just beyond this point and follows a ridge all the way down to the bottom. In the springtime, the hillside is a riot of balsamroot's yellow blooms, and the crazy-quilt colours of purple fleabane, yellow hedysarum, prairie groundsel, lupines, stickweed and pink pussytoes. At the end of the ridge, a short bushwhack to the right leads to a road that switchbacks past the farmstead toward Drum Creek. Cross the fence and turn left onto the Drum Creek road where there are the remains of a flume, a railway trestle across the creek and the concrete foundations of a weigh scale. After the creek crossing keep left on the main road, which takes you to the remains of the Hillcrest Coal and Coke Company's surface plant. Just beyond the remains of the largest structure, the power house, bear left. Keep left at the next three intersections and walk down to the streets of Hillcrest and your second vehicle.

*At the summit of Turtle Mountain.*

# Hillcrest

Located south of Highway 3 is the quiet residential area of Hillcrest. Never a large place, Hillcrest nonetheless reflects the town planning ideals of the early 20th century. The streets, despite topography, are laid out on a grid and the main street, 9 Avenue, was more than 24 m wide. Many of the homes and businesses you see when driving around the town pre-date the Second World War when the mine was still operational.

It was Charles (Chippy) Plummer Hill, an American entrepreneur, who prospected the coal seams around what is now Hillcrest at the turn of the 20th century. It took him three years before he had accumulated enough capital to open his mine, but on January 31, 1905, Hillcrest Coal and Coke Company began production. Like all the towns in the Crowsnest Pass, the village of Hillcrest was laid out and built immediately adjacent to the mine site. By 1910, when Hill sold his mine, Hillcrest boasted a spur rail line to the Canadian Pacific Railway, a train station, a school, a hotel and a store that still stands today at 22705 8 Avenue. In 1911 when a major strike closed the mine the new owners, Hillcrest Collieries, built a two-storey general office and several cottages for the mine officials. Only one of these buildings remains: the mine manager's house at the corner of 226 Street and 8 Avenue.

The mine at Hillcrest remained in business until 1939 when Hillcrest Collieries amalgamated with Mohawk to form Hillcrest Mohawk Collieries. It was at this point that work on the Hillcrest seams ceased and the townsite quietly retreated from the clamour of the coal industry.

In addition to the main Hillcrest townsite, there is a residential area called "Il Bosc" or Bushtown located north of the town near the railway tracks. Here, a small number of families lived from approximately 1910 to 1955. The homes were often made from salvaged lumber and everyone kept their own cows and chickens. When the boxcars lined the railway, the residents scoured them for any wheat, which was then swept up and taken home for chicken feed. They also scrounged the tracks for lumps of coal that fell out of the cars—a welcome gift to families who did not have a great deal of money.

*Hoist house No. 1, ca. 1920s after repairs. Courtesy Provincial Archives of Alberta, Archives Collection A 2417.*

# 40 HILLCREST CEMETERY

**Duration** half day
**Distance** 5.5 km return
**Level of Difficulty** Easy hike along four-wheel-drive roads. Open ridges and some bushwhacking.
**Maximum Elevation** 1616 m
**Elevation Gain** 335 m
**Map** Blairmore 82 G/9

## Access

From Highway 3 take the west access into Hillcrest along 9 Ave. Located a few hundred metres past the railway tracks is a fork. Take the left-hand fork to continue on 9 Ave. to 230 St. Turn right and park near the corner of 230 St. and 7 Ave. Your trailhead is the gravel road that leads uphill on the opposite side of the street.

A tremendous underground explosion tore through the Hillcrest mine on June 19, 1914, killing 189 men and boys. To help place the Hillcrest cemetery with its two large mass graves into context, this hike begins at the Hillcrest surface plant where you can still see evidence of the explosion. Then, to gain a bird's-eye perspective of the west shoulder of Hillcrest Mountain and of the Frank Slide, there is a tramp up a ridge. The hike ends with a visit to the cemetery.

Walk up the gravel road toward the Hillcrest surface plant. There are four forks. Bear right at all of them until you come to the remains of the surface plant (see plan on page 144). At the fifth fork, detour left for a short distance to view the hoist house that was blown apart by the impact of the 1914 explosion as it tore up No. 2 opening. Return to the main roadway and continue walking through the site to the remains of a flume, a railway trestle and the concrete foundation of a weigh scale at Drum Creek. Cross the creek and continue straight ahead on a pleasant old road heading toward the east flank of Turtle Mountain. At the top of a ridge, leave the road and bushwhack across to the next hillside to

*Mass graves at Hillcrest cemetery.*

## The Hillcrest Mine Disaster

On June 19, 1914, at 9:30 a.m., a tremendous explosion that a survivor later stated sounded "like the crack of a cannon, and without the slightest warning," shot through the tunnels of the Hillcrest mine. Such was the force of the explosion that above ground, the roof of the hoist house was blown 12 m off its foundation and its 20 cm-thick concrete walls smashed. The hoist engine itself was heavily damaged. Of the 237 men on shift that day, 189 died. The Hillcrest mine explosion remains the worst mining disaster in Canadian history.

The numbers might have been higher had it not been for the quick thinking of the general manager who immediately realized the consequences of such an explosion. Knowing that nearly all of the oxygen in the mine had been depleted and only deadly carbon monoxide and carbon dioxide remained, he raced to the fan house where he threw the engine in reverse to force fresh air down into the mine. Rescue operations commenced almost immediately. The previous year, a remodelled passenger coach purchased from the Canadian Pacific Railway had been converted into a mine rescue office where volunteers were given 10 days of intensive training in mine rescue techniques. Responding to the call for help, the Canadian Pacific Railway sent an engine from Fernie, British Columbia, to bring Mine Rescue No. 1, as the office was dubbed, to Hillcrest. Rescue crews armed with pulmotor equipment that gave artificial respiration raced to the scene. Friends and relatives lined the roadway, waiting. As the badly disfigured bodies were recovered and brought to the surface, they were taken to the wash house and checked for their number tag, which was the only method by which a body could be positively identified.

There was scarcely a house in Hillcrest that was not draped in black crepe in the days following the explosion. Hastily-built coffins were laid in two mass graves following days of funeral services. For the families, the death of a father or husband meant financial hardship and a relief fund for the stricken families was established to ease the financial blow.

The company worked quickly to bring the mine back into production. Suspecting the explosion was caused by falling rock, which in turn sparked the highly explosive coal dust, the company attempted to introduce locked safety lamps to replace the open flame lamps for its workers. Even though it was known the risk of an explosion was higher with open flame lamps and despite the incredible carnage caused by such an explosion, the Hillcrest miners went on strike demanding the removal of the safety lamps! They argued the weaker light given by the safety lamp was the more dangerous risk. Miners elsewhere demanded a raise in pay to compensate for having to use safety lamps.

Death returned to the Hillcrest mine 12 years later at 10:20 p.m. on September 19, 1926, when another explosion, even more destructive than that of 1914, ripped through the workings. Mine rails were twisted like pretzels, mine cars were smashed and timbers were ripped away as though they had not been there. Two men who were in the mine at the time were killed.

*Mass burial, June 1914. Courtesy Provincial Archives of Alberta, Archives Collection A 1781.*

*Waiting for the bodies. Courtesy Glenbow Archives, NA 629-1.*

the north, an open ridge that invites a break while you enjoy scenes of the Frank Slide, Hillcrest and Bellevue. Located directly below is a dirt track running south-southeast through a meadow to the Hillcrest cemetery.

To access the track, follow the ridge in a northerly direction to where it runs down slope. A short downhill bushwhack leads you to a cutline. Turn right and follow the cutline to the dirt track at a solitary spruce tree in the meadow. In early spring this meadow is a carpet of crocus. Turn right onto the track and cross a cattleguard. Just after crossing under a hydro line, at the bottom of a small slope, cut diagonally left across a small field and through a poplar stand. Cross a fence to what is marked on the topographic map as a slough, but that has now been drained. From here you can see the cemetery. Cross the cemetery fence. The Hillcrest cemetery, with its two large mass graves delineated by white picket fences, paints an especially poignant picture of life in a coal mining town in the Crowsnest Pass.

Walk eastward through the cemetery and out to the junction of 9 Avenue. Turn right and walk as far as 230 Street where you can pick up your vehicle nearby.

| | |
|---|---|
| 0 m | trailhead |
| 70 m | first fork |
| 300 m | second fork |
| 400 m | third fork and water tower |
| 600 m | fourth fork and surface plant |
| 700 m | fork |
| 1.0 km | flume and trestle and Drum Creek crossing |
| 1.8 km | first ridge |
| 2.5 km | track in valley floor |
| 3.4 km | Hillcrest Cemetery |
| 5.5 km | return to trailhead |

# 41 THE HILLCREST SEAM

This hike will introduce you to a major geological feature and the remains of Hillcrest Collieries surface plant.

Walk up the gravel road. There are four intersections en route to the surface plant. At the first two intersections, bear to the right. At the third intersection, take a short detour and go left past the concrete water tower to a distinct slack-strewn path that leads along the edge of the ridge overlooking Hillcrest as far as the concrete foundation of a conveyor that moved the coal to the tipple located at the base of the hill. Look down into the foundation and you can still see a screen that was used at this tipple. Return to the main track and bear to the left. Keep to the right at the next intersection to arrive at the ruins of several buildings associated with Hillcrest Collieries. Enough remains of the Hillcrest mine site for you to appreciate the above ground workings of this major mine. To your right are the walls of the power house, perhaps the most important support structure at any underground mine. The foundation between the road and the power house may be that of the wash house. Immediately across the road is

**Duration** 2 hours

**Distance** 4.9 km

**Level of Difficulty** Four-wheel-drive roads. Open slopes and some bushwhacking.

**Maximum Elevation** 1463 m

**Elevation Gain** 274 m

**Map** Blairmore 82 G/9

## Access

From Highway 3 take the west access into Hillcrest along 9 Ave. A few hundred metres past the railway tracks there is a fork. Take the left-hand fork to continue on 9 Ave. to 230 St. Turn right and park near the corner of 230 St. and 7 Ave. Your trailhead is the gravel road leading uphill from the opposite side of the street.

| | |
|---|---|
| 0 m | trailhead |
| 70 m | first fork |
| 300 m | second fork |
| 400 m | third fork and water tower |
| 600 m | fourth fork and surface plant |
| 700 m | fork |
| 1.0 km | first road crossing |
| 1.5 km | coal seam |
| 2.4 km | dirt bike path |
| 3.6 km | road |
| 4.2 km | surface plant |
| 4.3 km | fork |
| 4.5 km | fork |
| 4.6 km | fork and water tower |
| 4.8 km | fork |
| 4.9 km | trailhead |

*Mine opening en route to the exposed coal seam.*

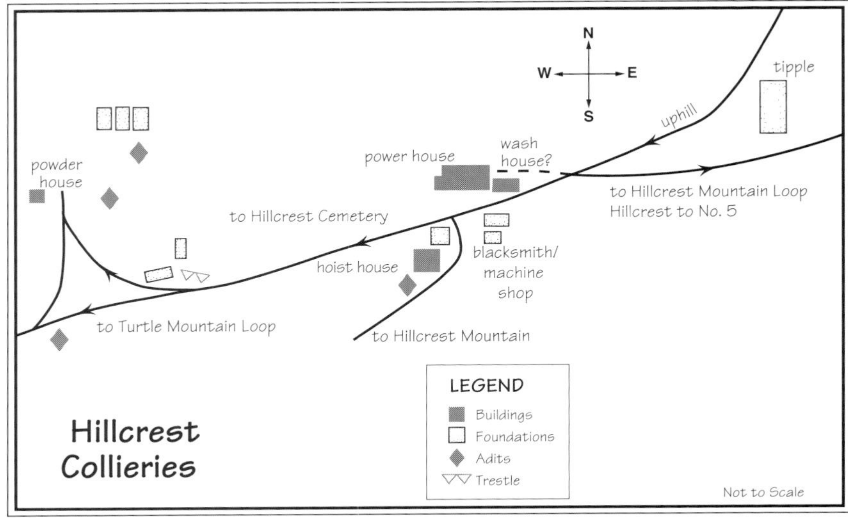


the foundation of the machine shop where all repairs to equipment were carried out.

Just past here, the road forks. Turn left. Forty metres beyond, go left at another fork and begin a short, steep ascent, ignoring an old mining road that crosses the path four times as it switchbacks to the top of the slope. Just before you reach the dramatic conclusion at the end, there are two openings on your right beneath an overhanging rock.

From here, it is only a short distance along the track before you reach its end at a magnificent, exposed coal seam where you can view the thickness and pitch of the seams worked by the Hillcrest miners. From the coal seam, a path continues climbing to a lookout point. The mountains of the Livingstone Range across the valley provide a backdrop for the seemingly tiny vehicles travelling along Highway 3. From here, the path enters a broad meadow on the east side of the shoulder of Hillcrest Mountain.

When halfway around the meadow take the dirt bike trail to the top of a shoulder of Hillcrest Mountain—a relatively steep climb to a rock outcropping. Swing to the right where the path disappears and continue uphill, following the ridge through the spruce copse to an open field. In front of you is the east flank of Turtle Mountain. To its right, the eastern edge of the Frank Slide can just be seen, while to the left the snow-covered peaks of the Flathead Range tower in the distance. The summit of Hillcrest Mountain on your left is hidden from view by intervening hilltops. Standing at 2164 m, it is named for the founder of the Hillcrest mines.

At the end of the meadow, bushwhack to the right. The lower part of the slope is crisscrossed by old mining roads. Take any one that leads downhill; they all lead to the surface plant. To access your vehicle, walk back down the road keeping left at all forks.

## Hillcrest Collieries

The first person to work these seams was C. P. (Chippy) Hill, an American entrepreneur. By January 31, 1905, Hill began to dig tunnels, secure timber and water rights, and build housing for the miners. He was faced with a small problem of how to move his coal 900 m from the mine opening close to his surface plant to the tipple at the bottom of the hill. He solved this by building a conveyor at the top of the hill. From the main tipple below, the coal was shipped along a 3.2 km-long standard gauge railway to the main line of the Canadian Pacific. Chippy liked to boast that although his railway was not as long as the Canadian Pacific Railway's, it was just as wide! At the tipple, the coal initially passed along a picking table where workers removed rock and other debris. Then, the coal moved over a series of screens, one of which you saw at the tipple site. The screens had different size holes, the holes decreasing in size as the coal moved along. All pieces of coal smaller than the hole fell through to the next screen where it was again sorted. Most tipples sorted coal according to lump, nut, pea and slack sizes. Hill knew the rich seams would produce some of the finest coal in the Rocky Mountains because of the high carbon content and low ash. And true to his expectations, once he was able to teach the engineers on the Canadian Pacific Railway steam engines how to fire his coal, the railway company reserved all Hillcrest coal for its passenger trains.

Labour disputes hampered the coal industry in the Crowsnest Pass almost from the beginning. Strikes over wages and working conditions caused work stoppages almost every second year from 1905 to 1932. In 1906-07, Hill attempted to break the power of the fledgling miners' union by cutting the men's pay from 55 cents to 45 cents a ton. When the miners protested, Hill closed the mine. Although he was eventually forced to back down on this issue, Hill's penchant for getting into trouble with the miners and their union followed him into 1908. Firing "agitators" from his mine, he argued for a payment of only 35 cents a ton, citing extra production costs of a muddy main entry, a costly haulage system and his 3.2 km-long spur line out to the Canadian Pacific Railway ought to exempt him from the rate of pay to which he had agreed in the last contract signed with the union.

*The ruins of Hillcrest power house.*

*Hillcrest miners with their horses, ca. 1924. Courtesy Provincial Archives of Alberta, Archives Collection A 2414.*

Another sore point with the miners was the wash house. Even before the law demanded companies provide wash and change facilities for their workers, Hill had provided a room over the boilers for the men. However, the boiler pipes passed through the floor where waste steam escaped. The heat was, no doubt, welcomed during the cold months, but the steam prevented wet clothes from drying. Also, when the boiler pipes were cleaned, soot and ash were spewed into the men's change room. Clearly, Hill's wash house was a "dirty, filthy hole [where]...no decent man would keep hogs in." Despite orders from provincial mines inspectors, Hill refused to provide new facilities for 16 long months before he capitulated.

Mine managers like Hill soon learned to use down time owing to strikes or poor markets to their advantage by improving their surface plant operations. When labour disputes disrupted work in 1908, Hill replaced his horse-drawn haulage system with a steam locomotive that pulled mine cars from the main entry to the tipple. Although it cost Hill over $100,000 to make these improvements, production rose from 30,000 tonnes in 1906 to 130,000 in 1908.

Most of the buildings you saw on this hike post-date Hill's involvement because in 1910, he sold his company to a Montreal syndicate that reorganized the mine under the name Hillcrest Collieries. When William Hutchinson, a surveyor-engineer with Hillcrest Collieries, first arrived at Hillcrest in May 1910, the company was mining only one seam, but it was 4.3 m thick! Hutchinson recalled the situation at the mine: "...the original mine office was still in use. It was a large log building situated on the north side of Hillcrest Creek, alongside of what was then the only wagon road to the mine. The stables and stable boss's house were to the west of the office and there were three or four small cottages east of it, in one of which the Mine Manager lived....This just about constituted the original Hillcrest mine lay-out. In the spring and summer of 1911 a number of new company buildings had been erected....These included a two-storey general office, a two-storey general manager's house and another smaller two storey house.... In the summer of 1911...the new power house had been erected and equipped and was now supplying power for all our mining and other operations."

Within a short time of opening No. 2 mine (the second of three rich seams), the mine was producing 2,000 tonnes of coal each day. It remained in business until 1939 when Hillcrest Collieries amalgamated with Mohawk to form Hillcrest Mohawk Collieries. It was at this point that work on the Hillcrest seams ceased.

# 42 HILLCREST MINE LOOP

**Duration** half day

**Distance** 7.6 km

**Level of Difficulty**
Straightforward hike on alternately soft and hard-packed four-wheel-drive roads.

**Maximum Elevation** 1372 m

**Elevation Gain** 213 m

**Map** Blairmore 82 G/9

## Access

From Highway 3 take the west access into Hillcrest along 9 Ave. A few hundred metres past the railway tracks there is a fork. Take the left-hand fork to continue on 9 Ave. to 230 St. Turn right and park near the corner of 230 St. and 7 Ave. Your trailhead is the gravel road leading uphill from the opposite side of the street.

| | |
|---|---|
| 0 m | trailhead |
| 70 m | first fork |
| 300 m | second fork |
| 400 m | third fork and water tower |
| 600 m | tipple remains |
| 800 m | fourth fork |
| 1.5 km | coal seam and fork |
| 2.4 km | dirt bike crossing |
| 2.8 km | stream |
| 3.4 km | two forks |
| 3.7 km | T-junction |
| 5.4 km | fork |
| 6.0 km | intersection with two roads |
| 6.9 km | surface plant |
| 7.0 km | fork |
| 7.2 km | fork and water tower |
| 7.3 km | fork |
| 7.5 km | fork |
| 7.6 km | trailhead |

In our opinion spring is the best time of year in the Crowsnest Pass when the profusion of wildflowers is nothing less than remarkable. This pleasant hike offers a lengthier circuit above the Hillcrest surface plant than the previous trail, "The Hillcrest Seam." It circles the northeast shoulder of Hillcrest Mountain via alternating meadow paths and forest roadways, then takes you through the surface plant of Hillcrest Collieries before returning to the trailhead.

Walk up the gravel road. At the first two intersections, bear to the right. At the third intersection, go left past the concrete water tower to a distinct slack-strewn path that leads along the edge of the ridge overlooking Hillcrest as far as the concrete foundation of the Hillcrest conveyor to the tipple that was located below. From the conveyor foundation follow a well-marked path uphill through a poplar grove. Keep right at an intersection. The path soon breaks out of the open forest into a broad meadow. From here, the path continues upward through pine and spruce stands, then enters another broad meadow covering the entire southeast flank of a shoulder of Hillcrest Mountain. In spring, the green of the eastern slopes of the Rockies contrasts sharply with the snow-covered mountain tops of Waterton National Park, which can just be seen to the south. What impressed us, though, was the flowers. Rarely do you see such a display of wildflowers as those found here in the spring. The hillside is a carpet of big, yellow blooms of countless balsamroots that almost hide the intense blue-purple shooting stars, the purplish-red blooms of the fuzzy old man's whiskers, the purple crocus, sky pilots and countless other species. Stick to the path. Ground-nesting birds favour the warm slope for their nests.

## Mountain Meadows

The Crowsnest Pass is a fascinating area botanically. The hikes in this book take you from the rolling foothills up through the montane and subalpine zones to the high alpine. The type of vegetation these ecoregions support changes with location. Elevation is one key factor. The lower mountain slopes of the montane region support forests of pine and spruce and open meadows on south-facing slopes. As you climb into the subalpine and alpine the forests become thin and stunted. Near the treeline the proud Engelmann spruce is dwarfed to a gnarled, low, shrub-looking tree called krummholz. In the alpine, with less soil and greater winds, they disappear completely.

Another factor determining the type of plants found in the pass is the direction the mountain slopes face. North-facing slopes receive much less direct sunlight and are more protected from the prevailing winds than south-facing slopes. Heavily-shaded forest floors support mosses and moisture-loving woodland flowers such as orchids. In contrast, south-facing slopes are often open and exposed to wind and sun. There are more varieties of wildflowers on south-facing slopes and you can spend considerable time trying to identify the wide variety that can be found here.

There is a third factor determining the type of plants that grow in the pass and that is climate. The higher you climb the cooler and shorter are the summers. Mountain avens and cinquefoils can be found along with heathers and moss campion. The warmer lower regions support different flowers such as balsamroot and crocus.

Another factor almost all plants found in the Front Ranges have in common is the chinook winds that can blow at gale-force through the mountain passes. It is not uncommon to drive through the Crowsnest Pass in the dead of winter with snow only being found at higher elevations.

Because the Crowsnest Pass serves as a transitional zone for floral species, some plants common in Waterton National Park and Montana to the south are not found north of the pass. Likewise, a number of species found in Banff National Park and Kananaskis Country are not found south of the Crowsnest Pass.

*Balsamroots. Photo Julie Hrapko.*

*Screen and picking table, 1912-14. Courtesy Glenbow Archives, NA 2889-41.*

Cross a dirt bike trail, and continue along a pleasant old road as it descends to a small stream. After crossing the stream and a meadow, keep right at an intersection with a grassy roadway. At another fork just a few metres beyond, keep to the right again, climbing slowly over the crest of a rise in the shade of poplar woods that provide welcome relief on a warm day. Shortly beyond the crest is a T-junction with the route to Hillcrest Mohawk No. 5.

To return to Hillcrest, turn right on a road that climbs over the brow of a hill, then descends with satisfying views across to Turtle Mountain. Continue to swing around the flank of Hillcrest Mountain to another fork at the bottom of a steep descent. Turn right. A short walk brings you to two intersections within metres of each other. At the first, go right. Ten metres later at the second fork, turn left and continue downhill to the surface plant. From the remains of the power house on your left, bear left at all intersections to return to your vehicle.

# 43 RIVER WALK

As either a restful evening stroll or as a fisherman's access to the Crowsnest River, this walk is more of a delight than the access would lead you to believe. The Mohawk cleaning plant that overlooks the Crowsnest River adds a historic note to an otherwise pastoral setting.

From the trailhead, a four-wheel-drive track leads to a cattle gate. Pass through and follow what is by now a hiking path down to the Crowsnest River passing through what used to be, up to 1955, "Il Bosc" or Bushtown where a number of families resided. In places, you can still find cellar depressions adjacent to the path.

Continue alongside the Crowsnest River where high banks across the river illustrate the folds and pitches resulting from the mountain building process. Sheltered from the strong winds that sometimes blow from the west, the trail leads past swimming and fishing holes where local residents can be seen trying their luck. Once well known for its stocks of bull trout (Dolly Varden) and cutthroat trout, the Crowsnest River, the Crowsnest Lake and other streams such as Gold Creek, which feed into the Crowsnest, are now bereft of many of these species. Mining, highway diversions, the Canadian

**Duration** 1 hour

**Distance** 2.4 km return

**Level of Difficulty** Easy walk on well-marked path.

**Maximum Elevation** 1250 m

**Elevation Gain** negligible

**Map** Blairmore 82 G/9

## Access

Turn off Highway 3 at the West Hillcrest access. Just before crossing the railway tracks, turn left onto 217 St. Looping around the residential area, the road climbs a small coal slack ridge and runs east to a fork in the road where, in front and above you, are the remains of the Mohawk cleaning plant. Park your vehicle here.

| | |
|---|---|
| 0 m | trailhead beneath the Mohawk cleaning plant |
| 100 m | cattle gate |
| 900 m | coal slack field and tributary to Crowsnest River |
| 1.2 km | end of trail |
| 2.4 km | return to trailhead |

*Dipping strata, looking south across the Crowsnest River.*

Pacific Railway's line and the Frank Slide have all contributed to their disappearance. On the other hand, rainbow trout introduced in the 1920s have done well and many of the fishermen at the Crowsnest River are fishing with rainbow in mind.

At 1.2 km from the trailhead, the hike ends at a tributary stream flowing into the Crowsnest River. Here, too, is a small quantity of coal slack from the mining operations that coloured this river flat for more than 40 years. If you wish, you can cross the stream and follow the trail eastward, but the path is heavily overgrown and to keep to the path you will be required to duck through shrubs and detour around wet areas. Daisies, asters and goldenrod keep you company along the entire way.

Return the way you came.

## Mohawk Bituminous Collieries

The high quality seams just east of West Canadian Collieries' Bellevue operation were exploited as early as 1907 by the Maple Leaf Coal Company. It built a tipple, a power house, a wash house, and a 12-horse stable and granary for the horses, which were used to haul coal cars to and from the mine, all by 1911 and at a cost of $30,000. The time and effort spent in developing the surface plant brought immediate results. Coal production increased from 15,000 tonnes in 1908 to nearly 50,000 tonnes each year thereafter until 1913. But the capital expenditures, along with an economic recession in 1908, a eight-month strike in 1911, and the destruction of the wash house by a fire caused by overheated pipes, strained the company's cash flow. Like a number of other companies and mines, Maple Leaf was forced out of operation by the onset of the First World War. The

*Cleaning plant at the Hillcrest Mohawk Collieries, 1945. Photo Thomas Gushul. Courtesy Glenbow Archives, NC 54-2889.*

Ruins of the Mohawk cleaning plant.

mine lay idle until 1919 when a new company, Bellevue Collieries, took over. Cancellation of Canadian Pacific Railway orders and water problems in the mine led to a reorganization and within a few months, a new company, Mohawk Bituminous Collieries, assumed ownership. The old Maple Leaf tipple, where all coal was cleaned and sorted, was upgraded during the 1920s. The high ash content of the coal made Mohawk's product undesirable to all customers for no one wanted "dirty" coal that did not burn cleanly, so the company installed a dry washery. It must have worked quite well because Mohawk was able to reclean an old stockpile of slack coal and sell it to the smelters in British Columbia.

The remains of the tipple that you parked beneath at the beginning of this hike date from the 1930s when Mohawk made a number of improvements to its surface plant in an effort to remain competitive. But the 1930s were not good years. Many mines laid off workers when orders were not forthcoming. Mohawk kept all 105 workers underground employed because "of the improbability of [the men] finding work anywhere else." In the end, the Depression was too much for the company and in 1939 it amalgamated with Hillcrest Mines. The new company, Hillcrest Mohawk, closed the aging Hillcrest mines and surface plant in favour of continuing work at the Mohawk seams. Demand for coal during the Second World War gave Hillcrest Mohawk Collieries Ltd. the boost it needed to survive. As well, a 15 cent increase in the price of a ton of coal gave the company more working capital. The Mohawk cleaning plant remained operational until it, too, was forced to close in 1952 when Hillcrest Mohawk merged with Consolidated Mining and Smelting of Coleman to form Coleman Collieries. Within two months, Coleman Collieries moved in, dismantling much of the Hillcrest Mohawk plant for salvage. These plans went awry in October, 1953, when a fire gutted the cleaning plant. Today, only the brick portion remains as testimony to the companies that worked the seams in this part of the pass.

# 44 HASTINGS RIDGE

This hike, which introduces you to an open pit mining operation, additionally offers spectacular views of the Lyons Creek valley, the Flatheads and the peaks of Waterton National Park.

From the T-junction, bear left and walk up the hard-packed road. At a fork, turn left and wind up to the top of Hastings Ridge, named by J. B. Tyrrell for Tom Hastings, a member of the 1884 geological survey party. This ridge witnessed frantic mining activity after the Second World War. The first hint of the richness of the coal seams becomes apparent when, breaking out of the forest, you find yourself suddenly perched at the edge of a huge slack pile. At a second fork, bear right and climb the slack for a magnificent view of the valley below and the mountain ranges to the south and west. Below is the deep pit where West Canadian Collieries extracted its coal.

Return to the T-junction and your vehicle.

**Duration** half day

**Distance** 3.6 km

**Level of Difficulty** Easy walk on four-wheel-drive roads.

**Maximum Elevation** 1908 m

**Elevation Gain** 100 m

**Map** Beaver Mines 82 G/8

## Access

From Highway 3 take the west access into Hillcrest along 9 Ave. A few hundred metres past the railway tracks there is a fork. Take the left-hand fork to continue on 9 Ave. to 230 St. Continue straight ahead onto 232 St. as it winds to the left and continues out of Hillcrest as far as the Lynx Creek Recreation sign. Turn right and drive up the Lynx Creek road for 9.2 km. Immediately past the

*View to the west of snow-covered peaks in the Flathead Range.*

cattleguard at the summit of the pass, turn right onto a mining road and drive another 2 km to a T-junction. Park here as the road beyond this point is only suitable for four-wheel-drive vehicles.

| | |
|---|---|
| 0 m | trailhead |
| 700 m | first fork |
| 1.1 km | second fork and open pit mine |
| 2.2 km | return to trailhead |
| 2.5 km | third fork |
| 2.6 km | fourth fork |
| 2.9 km | open pit mine |
| 3.6 km | return to trailhead |

*The worked seam at Hastings Ridge used on the descent.*

**Option** For a backside view of yet another open pit backdropped by the high rocky peaks of the Flathead Range, continue to walk straight ahead. Turn left at a fork in the road and go as far as another fork 100 m beyond. Keep left. As you approach the top of the ridge, the old road swings to the south-southwest, offering terrific views of Willoughby Ridge and the Flathead Range, then leads down to the backside of another open pit. A scramble up the side of the opened seam to the top gives you an appreciation for the techniques involved in open pit mining. For a fun return to the road, descend into the worked seam and follow it down through the slack to the road.

Return the way you came.

# 45 ADANAC RIDGE

This invigorating hike leads from the top of an unnamed pass on the Lynx Creek road north along Adanac Ridge to the Adanac mine site. Glorious views to the north, east and west accompany you all the way.

From the trailhead follow the four-wheel-drive track up the hill on the east side of the road. It is a longer and steeper pull to the top of the ridge than you at first realize, but the vista of rolling green foothills and prairie to the east, the Livingstone Range to the north, the Flathead Range to the west and the mountains of Waterton National Park to the south makes the climb worthwhile.

Turn left to go downhill. The way down the ridge is along the spine of the ridge. It is an easy walk and one that is open with only two small spruce copses to block your path. At the extreme northerly end of the spine you must descend the ridge via the steep west slope. At the top the footing is tricky owing to scree, and near the bottom you must bushwhack through poplar and spruce bush. When you reach the bottom of Adanac Ridge you find yourself among the remains of West Canadian Collieries' Adanac mine.

From the mine site, walk down the mine road to the Lynx Creek road. To return to your car, turn left and walk up the road to the top of the pass.

**Duration** half day
**Distance** 7.1 km return
**Level of Difficulty** Moderately steep climb on four-wheel-drive road. Descent has scree and short sections of bushwhacking.
**Maximum Elevation** 1921 m
**Elevation Gain** 213 m
**Elevation Loss** 427 m
**Maps** Blairmore 82 G/9
Beaver Mines 82 G/8

## Access

From Highway 3 take the west access into Hillcrest along 9 Ave. A few hundred metres past the railway tracks there is a fork. Take the left-hand fork to continue on 9 Ave. to 230 St. Continue straight ahead onto 232 St. as it winds to the left and continues out of Hillcrest as far as the Lynx Creek Recreation sign. Turn right and drive up the Lynx Creek road for 9.2 km. Located immediately past the cattleguard at the summit of the pass is a turnout. Park here.

| | |
|---|---|
| 0 m | trailhead |
| 600 m | top of the ridge |
| 3.7 km | surface plant |
| 4.9 km | start of bushwhack to hard rock opening |
| 5.4 km | hard rock opening |
| 7.1 km | return to second vehicle |

*Coal chute.*

*View from the ridge looking southwest toward the snow-covered peaks of Waterton National Park.*

## The Adanac Mine

When West Canadian Collieries began operation in 1903, it was convinced of its future in the Crowsnest Pass, and leased more than 29,000 ha of land, including the Adanac Ridge. The success of its Greenhill, Lille and Bellevue mines meant the company did not need to exploit the Adanac seams until the autumn of 1941 when, after a long decline in coal markets, the Second World War brought a sudden demand for good steam coal. Discovering a 4.3 m-thick seam, the company undertook serious development the following year. First, the Adanac road was built and coal storage bins erected. The storage bins were necessary for no tipple was ever constructed at Adanac; instead, all Adanac's coal was screened and washed at the main Bellevue mine. Adanac was one of the last and most modern underground mines in the pass. Cutting machines were used at the coal face instead of picks and axes, and the entire mine underground was electrified. In a matter of 15 years, West Canadian Collieries extracted 641,000 tonnes of coal from this ridge. But modernization underground did not prevent the inevitable decline following peace in 1945. The mine closed in 1957 and the company went out of business in 1962.

# 46 HILLCREST MOHAWK NO. 5

This pleasant road winds uphill to No. 5 mine site of Hillcrest Mohawk Collieries, then continues to a ridge with a 360 degree vista. The climb to the ridge top is relatively steep and can be tiring on a hot day, but the views make it well worthwhile.

If you have two cars, consider following the option to Hillcrest Collieries surface plant. The last few kilometres follows "Hillcrest Mine Loop."

From the trailhead walk uphill along the four-wheel-drive road. Along the way to the surface plant there are several secondary trails branching off, but ignore all of them and continue climbing for approximately 2 km to the remains of a timber tipple. Located just above the tipple are several other mine structures and foundations.

From the tipple, walk up an increasingly rough road that heads toward the saddle on a shoulder of Hillcrest Mountain. The last part of the road switchbacks steeply, but the views from the open ridge are well worth the effort. On one side you can see Bellevue, Hillcrest and the prairie beyond, and on the other views toward Waterton National Park and Montana.

**Duration** 2.5 hours
**Distance** 7.4 km return
**Option** 8.9 km
**Level of Difficulty** Easy walk on hard-packed road with optional ridge descent. Option follows trails and old roads.
**Maximum Elevation** 1829 m
**Elevation Gain** 305 m
**Map** Blairmore 82 G/9

## Access

From Highway 3 take the west access into Hillcrest along 9 Ave. A few hundred metres past the railway tracks there is a fork. Take the left-hand fork to continue on 9 Ave. to 230 St. Continue straight ahead onto 232 St. as it winds to the left and continues

*Dynamite shed.*

# Hillcrest Mohawk No. 5 Mine

As early as 1907, Maple Leaf mine at Bellevue was interested in this site. But it was not until the demand for coal created by the Second World War, which rendered markets stronger than they had been for a number of years, that Hillcrest Mohawk in 1944 began operating what turned out to be its last underground mine. The company had originally thought of trucking the coal back to its tipple near Bellevue, but because of the cost decided to build a wooden tipple here instead. Surface plant operations were in full swing by 1946 with the construction of a rock and coal bin, a wash house, offices, a lamp house and a compressor house. A line was cut through heavy bush to bring in electricity, the cost of which was shared by West Canadian Collieries, which also required electricity for its Adanac mine across the valley. Although intended to replace the aging Bellevue mine, No. 5 mine did not prove profitable for Hillcrest Mohawk. The seams are nearly vertical, making "room and pillar" mining exceptionally dangerous. Also, although it appeared the seams would yield high quality coal, they were faulted and irregular. An unusually high amount of water in the mine further complicated the miners' work, which, according to the district inspector of mines in 1951, led a number of disgruntled miners to look for other jobs in the Crowsnest Pass. When the company was forced by economic reasons to merge with McGillivray-International of Coleman in 1952, the new company, Coleman Collieries, closed No. 5 in early 1952 by first removing the rails and hoist and then by dismantling the tipple. Seven years of operation, though, had resulted in 4,684.8 tonnes of coal being extracted from this ridge.

*Hillcrest Mohawk No. 5 surface operations, August 19, 1949. Courtesy Provincial Archives of Alberta, Harry Pollard Collection P 876.*

Before returning to your vehicle, poke around the saddle where deep subsidence pits were fenced by Hillcrest Mohawk upon withdrawal from this site. The subsidence, no doubt, is owing to the collapse of the fragile roof over the steeply-pitched seams. There is also what appears to be a small quarry.

Return to the tipple by trotting down the open ridge. From here, you can descend to the tipple and follow the road back to your car, or for those of you who prefer a pleasant bushwhack, continue down the hillside, bearing to the left around the shoulder of the hill. This brings you back above the Lynx Creek road and your car.

**Option—Hillcrest Surface Plant**

From the saddle descend the steep rough road down the backside of the shoulder, passing stockpiled timbers and the remains of a ventilation fan associated with Hillcrest Mohawk Collieries and dating from 1944-1952. At the bottom of the hill the road makes a sharp 90 degree turn to the right. Beyond the small clearing it crosses a small stream, then climbs up to a T-junction. Bear right. Within a short distance there are two roads that join from the right. Ignore both and continue along the main road that crosses a small meadow. After crossing another small stream, the road, now a path, ascends the southeast flank of Hillcrest Mountain across a broad meadow covered with a wide variety of wildflowers in spring. If you are lucky, you will catch mule deer and elk browsing. Ignore an intersecting dirt bike path halfway through the meadow. The trail continues to climb, then swings to the northwest with views of Bellevue, Hillcrest, Highway 3 and the Livingstone Range.

The path now descends through open woodland to a magnificent exposed coal seam and a fork. Go to the right and head downhill through another meadow and mixed forest to an intersection. Keep left here and emerge on the lip of a ridge overlooking the town of Hillcrest. A concrete foundation on your right is the remains of the conveyor above the tipple at the Hillcrest Collieries.

Follow the slack-strewn path to a concrete water tower at a junction with an old road. Turn right downhill. Keep left at the next two junctions. Your second vehicle will be waiting at the bottom of the hill.

out of Hillcrest as far as the Lynx Creek Recreation sign. Turn right and drive up the Lynx Creek road for 3.7 km to where a rough gravel road leads to the right. Park here.

**Option**

From Highway 3 at the west access into Hillcrest drive your second vehicle along 9 Ave. A few hundred metres past the railway tracks turn left at a fork and continue along 9 Ave. to 230 St. Turn right and park near the corner of 230 St. and 7 Ave.

| | |
|---|---|
| 0 m | trailhead |
| 2.1 km | Hillcrest Mohawk surface plant |
| 3.7 km | top of the ridge |
| 7.4 km | return to trailhead |

**Option**

| | |
|---|---|
| 4.6 km | fan house |
| 5.1 km | stream crossing |
| 5.2 km | intersection |
| 5.5 km | two forks |
| 6.1 km | stream crossing |
| 6.5 km | dirt bike crossing |
| 7.3 km | coal seam and fork |
| 8.1 km | fork |
| 8.3 km | tipple |
| 8.5 km | intersection near water tower |
| 8.6 km | fork |
| 8.8 km | fork |
| 8.9 km | second vehicle |

# 47 BYRON HILL

The highest point around for some distance, Byron Hill gives fine views of the Flathead and High Rock ranges to the west as well as of the Livingstone Range to the north. The lower portion of this hike is through open woodlands that abound in wildflowers in the spring. A visit to an old mine site adds interest.

**Duration** half day

**Distance** 11.0 km return

**Level of Difficulty** Significant elevation gain on hard-packed roads leading to open ridges. Some bushwhacking at the beginning of the hike.

**Maximum Elevation** 1820 m

**Elevation Gain** 579 m

**Map** Blairmore 82 G/9

## Access

From Highway 3 drive 1.2 km down the Hillcrest east access road. Park on the north side of the bridge at a widening in the pavement.

From your vehicle walk to the south side of the bridge and scramble down the embankment to the confluence of Byron Creek with the Crowsnest River. Hop across Byron Creek and turn right to bushwhack upstream as far as an old roadway. Continue straight ahead ignoring the track on the left. Follow the road upward, skirting an impressive coal slack pile. At the top of the slack pile, two roads join from the left, but ignore these and continue along the main road if you are in a hurry to reach Byron Hill.

However, if you wish to explore this old mine site, a poke about the slack will reveal a few interesting features: a collapsed mine entry at the top of the slack and tipple foundations at the bottom and another collapsed entry located farther east near the bend in the Crowsnest River.

*Krummholz on Byron Hill.*

## The Byron Creek Mine

The two mine entries that you explored at the beginning of the hike date from different time periods and from different companies. This was not unusual; often a mining company made an entry only to abandon it for any number of reasons. Sometimes there was too much rock in the coal, or the coal had a high ash content that reduced its value. Or, perhaps, the seam simply pinched out. Then, later, the seam was reworked by a completely different company.

The first company attempting to exploit the coal along Byron Creek was Leitch Collieries Ltd. in 1907. Its assay reports showed the seam here was of high quality steam coal. Billy Hamilton, the mine manager and initiator, and his investors, the Leitch family, undertook a cautious development. Despite this approach, they nevertheless had to erect a wooden tipple, repair shops, supply storage and a spur rail line to the Canadian Pacific Railway—a sizeable outlay of money for cautious investors! The company drove a tunnel 914 m into the slope. Despite the fact the seam was initially 2 m wide, Leitch and Hamilton had their hopes dashed within a few years when the coal quality proved lower than first believed. Refusing to give up, they relocated farther north at the present-day Leitch Collieries Provincial Historic Site on Highway 3.

Undisturbed for years, the coal seam was tested once again, this time by Byron Creek Collieries in 1927. Hoping to expand its holdings, the company installed a wash house, two electric hoists and a fan before seam difficulties forced the company to abandon the property in 1931.

## Krummholz

Wind is a factor with which all living things have to contend in the Crowsnest Pass. It often blows very strongly and there is no better evidence of its constant presence than the shapes of the spruce trees that grow on the higher ridges such as Byron Hill. Unable to withstand the force of the wind, the trees are compelled to grow horizontally instead of vertically.

Krummholz are often denude of many needles, giving the spruce trees a grotesque appearance. The trees' bare limbs are a result of ice crystals sitting on top of the snow that has been whipped up by winter winds. Their abrasion rips off needles from all branches unprotected by a thick layer of snow.

## Byron Hill

This 1820 m-high hill is named for Frank Byron, an American prospector who scouted the Crowsnest Pass for gold, coal, anything he could claim, prior to the construction of the Canadian Pacific Railway line in 1898.

From the mine, the road climbs gently through spruce and pine forest paralleling Byron Creek on your right. At yet another fork, bear to the right and cross over a fence. From here, the rough road becomes a soft, needle-strewn pathway. If you wish to view the Byron Creek valley, walk through the open woodland to the right.

At a crossroads continue straight ahead. Within 600 m there is another fence crossing and a small stream crossing. Shortly beyond the stream, the old roadway makes a 90 degree turn to the left. Climbing steadily, you will cross another small tributary stream and some 600 m later arrive at a major intersection. Continue straight ahead but glance back over your shoulder to take in excellent views of Hillcrest Mountain and Bellevue. You can expect a steep climb from here to the top of the ridge. Scramble up a rocky outcropping above the road to the ridge top, which affords views of Turtle and Bluff mountains and the Frank Slide to the west. To the south are Hastings Ridge and the snow-topped summits of the Flathead Range. The plains toward Pincher Creek lie to the east.

The roadway continues on the lee side of the top of the mountain to a T-junction with a cutline. Go straight ahead, cross over the fence and take the four-wheel-drive track to the top of Byron Hill, which is marked by a white surveyor's stake.

Ridge systems to the south entice you to continue your tramp, but head southwest and trot down the open slope to a gravel road. At the bottom of the hill you have a short bushwhack through pine and spruce and a climb over a fence before reaching the road. Turn right and follow it up to a crossroads. Turn right again and climb steeply to the T-junction below the surveyor's marker. Bear left and return the way you came.

| | |
|---|---|
| 0 m | trailhead |
| 250 m | fork |
| 350 m | second and third forks |
| 450 m | fourth fork and fence |
| 1.2 km | crossroads |
| 1.6 km | stream |
| 2.0 km | tributary |
| 2.6 km | intersection |
| 3.7 km | top of ridge |
| 4.2 km | top of Byron Hill |
| 4.5 km | T-junction |
| 5.0 km | surveyor's stake |
| 5.5 km | gravel road |
| 6.2 km | crossroads |
| 6.7 km | T-junction |
| 11.0 km | trailhead |

# 48 BURMIS MINE RIDGE

**Duration** 2 hours

**Distance** 7 km return

**Level of Difficulty** Moderate elevation gain on trails following open ridges.

**Maximum Elevation** 1555 m

**Elevation Gain** 244 m

**Map** Blairmore 82 G/9

## Access

From Highway 3 drive 2 km south on Secondary Road 507 to a junction. Turn right to the Hiawatha Campground and park at its west end.

**Note**: As this is a private campground, there is a charge to gain access to the trailhead.

| | |
|---|---|
| 0 m | trailhead |
| 300 m | fork |
| 800 m | creek |
| 1.1 km | 90° turn |
| 1.8 km | stream crossing |
| 2.0 km | first meadow |
| 2.3 km | fork |
| 2.4 km | stream crossing |
| 2.7 km | second meadow |
| 3.0 km | top of the ridge |
| 3.5 km | top of mountain |
| 7.0 km | return to trailhead |

The mountains of the eastern portal with their evergreen-covered slopes appear far less interesting than those farther west. Consequently, this hike to a ridge top with superb views reached with very little effort is a very pleasant surprise. It also takes you close to the old Burmis mine that operated from 1924 to 1926 and again from 1961 to 1962.

Ignore a hiking trail sign just a few metres west of your parked vehicle. Instead, follow a rough gravel road heading west. At the fork in the road, continue straight ahead and down to an unnamed creek with its delightful little waterfall. The road, which now changes to a broad, grassy walkway, sweeps along the left bank of the stream for 300 m, then with a sharp 90 degree turn, climbs steeply to the top of a ridge. Jump over a small stream. As you pass through spruce and lodgepole pine woodlands keep a sharp eye open for mule deer.

The path soon breaks out of the forest onto a broad meadow. In the springtime, delicate silky lupines, shooting stars and blue beardtongues share the open slope with balsamroots, meadow parsnips and golden bean flowers. Views of the mountains to the west inspire you to continue climbing for what promises to be a superb sight from the top.

At a fork bear left and go downhill to cross a small stream. Three hundred metres beyond the stream, you reach a second meadow where the trail winds up around a rock outcropping. Past this point, the path is indistinct, but continue climbing, keeping slightly to the left, and you will soon see the track reappear to the left of another rock outcropping. Above you, the ridge beckons. Once you reach the ridge top, the route to the summit is clear. Follow the trail south along the spine, climbing through low bush cranberry, juniper and stands of pine. From the broad summit, you are greeted by a complete 360 degree view. To the south are the snow-covered peaks of Waterton National Park, to the west is the Flathead Range and to the north the limestone wall of the Livingstone Ridge. Out of view below you at the base of the hill is an opening for the old Burmis mine. To learn more about this mine refer to

Horses were used for underground haulage at some mines until the Second World War. Courtesy Provincial Archives of Alberta, Public Affairs Bureau Collection PA 1983/5.

"Burmis" on page 14. To the east, the plains stretch out and on a clear day you can see the town of Pincher Creek, which has an interesting story behind its name. Apparently, prospectors from Montana camped at the spot sometime in the 1860s and lost two pairs of pincers, which were found many years later by a North West Mounted Police detachment in 1875. The stream and later the town took the name of Pincher Creek.

Return the way you came.

## ACKNOWLEDGMENTS

The authors would like to gratefully acknowledge: Historic Sites Service's Research files and the Inventory of Potential Historic Sites, and the Provincial Museum of Alberta, Archaeological Survey, without which the unique approach to this book could not have been accomplished; Dan Kyba for technical advice and help; Steven Struthers for legal advice; Keith Gladwynn of the Energy Utilities Board for help in identifying mine sites; the Crowsnest Museum for allowing us to peruse its photographic files; Julie Hrapko, botanist, and Ron Mussieux, geologist, Provincial Museum of Alberta, for their help in their respective fields. And a special thanks to Gwen Chrapko for providing a warm place to sleep and to "Burt," who almost made it across every stream he attempted. To all, "thank you."

**Map Credits**: Hannah Aaron for the mine maps.

**Photo Credits**: Archival photographs from the Glenbow Archives in Calgary, the Provincial Archives of Alberta and the Provincial Museum of Alberta in Edmonton were used to enhance the text, as well as the Department of National Defense and Maureen Lowe. Contemporary photographs by Gillean and Tony Daffern, Julie Hrapko, Roy Mussieux and Michelle Tracy are credited where appropriate. All other photographs in this book were taken by the authors.

# Further Reading


**History**

*Crowsnest and Its People* vols. 1 and 2, n.p. Crowsnest Pass Historical Society, 1979.

*Crowsnest Pass Historical Driving Tour: Bellevue and Hillcrest, Blairmore, Coleman.* Edmonton: Alberta Culture and Multiculturalism, The Coal Association of Canada, Crowsnest Pass Ecomuseum Trust, 1990.

Babaian, Sharon from research papers by Lorry Felske. *The Coal Mining Industry in the Crow's Nest Pass.* Edmonton: Alberta Culture, Historic Sites Service, 1985.

Dawson, J. Brian. *Crowsnest: An Illustrated History and Guide to the Crowsnest Pass.* Vancouver: Altitude Publishing, 1995.

Karamitsanis, Aphrodite. *Place Names of Alberta: Volume I - Mountains, Mountain Parks and Foothills.* Calgary: Alberta Culture and Multiculturalism and Friends of Geographical Names of Alberta Society and University of Calgary Press, 1991.

**Flora and Fauna**

Droppo, Olga. *A Field Guide to Alberta Berries.* Calgary: Calgary Field Naturalists' Society, 1988.

McKenny Margaret and Daniel Stuntz. *The New Savory Wild Mushroom.* n.p. University of Washington Press, 1987.

Scotter, George W., Tom Ulrich and Edgar Jones. *Birds of the Canadian Rockies.* Saskatoon: Western Producer Prairie Books, 1990.

Scotter, George W. and Halle Flygare. *Wildflowers of the Canadian Rockies.* Edmonton: Hurtig Publishers, 1986.

Walker, Marilyn. *Harvesting the Northern Wild.* Yellowknife: The Northern Publishers, 1984.

Willard, Terry. *Edible and Medicinal Plants of the Rocky Mountains and Neighbouring Territories.* Calgary: Wild Rose College of Natural Healing, 1992.

**Geology**

Beaty, Chester B. *The Landscapes of Southern Alberta: A Regional Geomorphology.* n.p. University of Lethbridge, 1975.

Canadian Society of Petroleum Geologists. *Field Guide to Rock Formations of Southern Alberta (Stratigraphic Sections Guidebook).* n.p. 1978.

*Dictionary of Geological Terms: Revised Edition.* New York: Anchor Books, 1976.

Gadd, Ben. *Handbook of the Canadian Rockies.* Jasper: Corax Press, 1986.

Gladwynn, Keith. "Coal Atlas of Alberta: Operating and Abandoned Coal Mines in Alberta," Energy Resources Conservation Board, 1985.

Gordy, P. L., F. R. Frey and D. K. Norris. "Geological Guide for the CSPG 1977 Waterton-Glacier Park Field Conference," Canadian Society of Petroleum Geologists, Calgary, 1977.

Horenstein, Sidney. *Familiar Fossils.* New York: Alfred A. Knopf Inc., 1988.

Mussieux, Ron and Marilyn Nelson. *A Traveller's Guide to Geological Wonders in Alberta.* n.p. Canadian Society of Petroleum Geologists, Federation of Alberta Naturalists and The Provincial Museum of Alberta, 1998.

Thompson, Peter (ed). *Cave Exploration in Canada: A Special Issue of The Canadian Caver Magazine.* Edmonton: Department of Geography, University of Alberta, 1976.

# Glossary

**adit** - mine entrance

**afterdamp** - a dangerous mixture of gases left in coal mines after an explosion of firedamp.

**anticline** - an arch of stratified rock in which the layers slope downward in opposite directions from the centre.

**bituminous** - a rank of coal. Rank depends on the age of the coal; the younger the coal, the softer it is. In Alberta, rank also depends on location. The softest, youngest coals are found on the plains. Harder coals such as those of bituminous or anthracite rank are found only in the mountains.

**brattice cloth** - a nonporous material used to direct air up one side of a "room," across the coal face and down the other side.

**coke** - a fuel made from coal by heating it in an oxygen-reduced oven until all the gases have been burned off.

**colliery** - a coal mine with its buildings and equipment.

**entry** - access into the mine. The main entry was the largest, most heavily supported by timbers and was the entry along which the haulage system moved and the air, fresh or foul, flowed. The other entries, called counter entries, led to the miners' workplaces.

**fan house** - necessary for all mines, fan houses were installed above the seams either to inject fresh air or to suck out stale air. The flow of air swept away lethal methane gas that seeped from the coal face and, thus, helped to minimize the risk of a gas explosion. Early mines in the Crowsnest Pass relied on "natural" ventilation from ventilation shafts dug at intervals along a seam. But the extremely hazardous conditions of mining the pass coal owing to the presence of gas meant that as soon as companies were in a financial position to do so, they built fan houses at the intake and outflow. The first fans were exhaust fans, but at later dates all mines used fresh air fans.

**fault** - when rock does not withstand internal pressures that are part of the mountain-building process, it breaks or fractures, one part shifting either up or down in relation to the other. As the parts continue to slip past each other, whole mountains or ranges can move several kilometres.

**firedamp** - a mixture of gases, consisting mainly of methane, that forms in coal mines.

**flume** - a large inclined trough for carrying water.

**fold** - in the mountain-building process, rock is subjected to great pressures. Sometimes the rock will bend, resulting in folding.

**methane gas** - a colourless, odorless flammable gas.

**open pit mining** - surface mining in which the coal is exposed by removal of overburden.

**power house** - the building that supplies all the power to run both the surface and underground operations of a coal mine.

**pulmotor equipment** - Pulmotor was a trademark for a device used to restore natural breathing in persons rescued from mine disasters.

**prospect** - mineral property not yet productive.

# Glossary

**room and pillar** - a system of mining steeply pitched coal seams. The miners drove their rooms, or workplaces up the seam often at difficult angles. The rooms, carved out of the coal seam, were 3 to 5 m wide and were separated from each other by 15 m-wide pillars of coal. Once they had reached the end of the seam, the miners worked their way back down the seam extracting as much coal from the pillars as possible without collapsing the roof over themselves. Owners knew that "room and pillar" was wasteful, but had little choice.

**rotary dump** - a mechanism that turned coal cars, once inside the tipple, upside down to empty their load onto a conveyor system. The Greenhill mine was one of the few mines in the Crowsnest Pass that used this system.

**saddle notch corners** - on log buildings, overlapping end joints where the upper log has a semi-circular notch cut out for the receptacle of the lower log.

**scree** - a steep slope of loose rock often at the base of a cliff.

**sedimentary rock** - a layered rock that is composed of fragments of older rock or organic materials.

**shaft** - a deep passage dug from the surface into a mine.

**sinkhole** - a hollow place where water collects.

**slack** - dirt, coal dust and small pieces of coal left after coal has been screened.

**steam coal** - a rank and size of coal suitable for firing the steam engines of early railway engines.

**subsidence** - is caused by the collapse of the roof over the mining tunnels. In the Crowsnest Pass, roofs are often weak owing to the method of "room and pillar" mining in which large pillars of coal are left supporting the roof while the miners worked the seam. Once they reached the end of a seam, the miners retreated and in so doing, took as much coal from the pillars as possible. The result was a weakened roof that over time collapses.

**syncline** - a downward fold of stratified rock in which the layers slope upward in opposite directions from the centre.

**talus** - a scree slope.

**tarn** - a small mountain lake.

**tipple** - building where the coal was sorted according to size.

**thrust** - an overriding movement of one crustal unit over another.

**thrust faulting** - a fault with a dip of less than 45° over much of its extent on which the hanging wall appears to have moved upward relative to the footwall.

**ventilation shaft** - a shaft dug directly over a seam to provide fresh air in the mine.

**washery** - used to clean slack coal before it was sent to the coking ovens. Some washeries were dry. Wet washeries used flotation to separate and clean the coal from ash and other impurities.

**wash house** - a separate building at the surface plant where the miners showered and changed their clothing before and after shift.

# *Useful Information*

## *TOURIST ATTRACTIONS*

Recognition of the Crowsnest Pass' unique heritage by both government and residents has resulted in the development of a number of attractions, listed below. There is often an admission charge.

### BURMIS

**The Leitch Collieries Provincial Historic Site**

Community Development has stabilized the ruins of this important pre-First World War colliery. Self-guiding trail as well as interpretive staff.

Dates: 15 May - Labour Day weekend
Hours: 9:00 am - 5:00 pm
Location: Highway 3 west of Burmis

### BELLEVUE

**Bellevue Mine**

The Crowsnest Pass Ecomuseum Trust has opened 366 m of the former West Canadian Collieries mine for guided tours. Temperature is approximately 7°C, so wear warm clothing and sturdy shoes.

Dates: end of June - 1 September
Hours: Wednesday - Sunday 10:00 am - 5:30 pm on the half hour
Location: from the corner of 213 Street and 25 Avenue, follow the signs that lead down the hill.

### FRANK

**CNP Allied Arts Association**

The pass' arts association and gallery offers exhibitions in all mediums of southern Alberta artists, art classes and coffee house entertainment every Wednesday at 7:00 p.m.

Hours: Tuesday - Friday 12:00 pm - 7:00 pm, closed 3 - 4:00 pm, Saturday 10:00 am - 4:00 pm, closed 12:30 - 1:30 pm, Sunday 12:00 pm - 4:00 pm
Location: Highway 3 in Frank

**The Frank Slide Interpretive Centre**

Community Development operates this interpretive centre on the history of the Crowsnest Pass. Includes the award-winning show "In The Mountain's Shadow." Historical vignettes presented.

Dates: year round
Hours: 24 May - Labour Day 9:00 am - 8:00 pm
Location: 1.5 km north of Highway 3 at Frank. Follow the signs.

### COLEMAN

**Allison Brood Trout Station**

Station provides eggs for fish hatcheries. Tours given during summer months.

Dates: long weekend in May - Labour Day weekend
Hours: 9:30 - 12:00 am and 1:00 - 3:30 pm. Closed weekends.
Location: Allison Creek recreation area on Allison Creek road west of Coleman.

**Crowsnest Museum**

Exhibits on mining, logging, early schools and businesses in the Crowsnest Pass are presented as well as an outdoor artifact garden.

Dates: year round
Hours: summer daily 10:00 - 4:00 pm
winter Monday - Friday 10:00 - 12:00 am and 1:00 - 4:00 pm
Location: 7701-18 Avenue

## *EATERIES*

### BELLEVUE

**Bellevue Restaurant**
2438-213 Street

### BLAIRMORE

**Cosmopolitan Inn**
13001-20 Avenue

**Highwood Motel**
11373-20 Avenue

**Kentucky Fried Chicken**
11913-20 Avenue

**King's Restaurant**
13249-20 Avenue

**Pixie Bar Drive Inn**
west end, 20 Avenue

**Rendez-Vous Restaurant**
13609-20 Avenue

**Something More in Dining**
Crowsnest Mall, east entrance

**Subway Sandwich & Salad**
8525-20 Avenue

**Yummy Inn Family Dining**
12337-20 Avenue

### COLEMAN

**Chris & Irvin's Cafe**
7802-17 Avenue

**Popiel's Family Restaurant**
Highway 3, Coleman

**Vito's Family Restaurant**
8505-20 Avenue

### CROWSNEST

**Inn on the Border**
Alberta-B.C. border

### HILLCREST

**Dee Dee's Deli**
22721-8 Avenue

## *PUB CRAWLS*

**Bellevue Inn**
2420-213 Street, Bellevue

**The Royal Canadian Legion**
2401-213 Street, Bellevue

**Best Canadian Motor Inn**
11217-20 Avenue, Blairmore

**Greenhill Hotel**
12326-20 Avenue, Blairmore

**London Arms Pub**
Highwood Motel
11373-20 Avenue, Blairmore

**Minesweepers Lounge**
2132-129 Street, Blairmore

**The Royal Canadian Legion**
12943-20 Avenue, Blairmore

**Tom's Tavern**
Cosmopolitan Inn
13001-20 Avenue, Blairmore

**The Grand Union Hotel**
7719-17 Avenue, Coleman

**The Royal Canadian Legion**
7831-17 Avenue, Coleman

## *ACCOMMODATION*

### BELLEVUE

**Bellevue Inn**
2420-213 Street
Tel: 564-4676

### BLAIRMORE

**Best Canadian Motor Inn**
11217-21 Avenue
Tel: 562-8851

**Celtic Croft Bed & Breakfast**
P.O. Box 52
Tel: 628-2393

**Cosmopolitan Inn**
13001-20 Avenue
Tel: 562-7321

**Greenhill Hotel**
12326-20 Avenue
Tel: 562-2232

**Hearthside Bed & Breakfast**
12313-21 Avenue
Tel: 562-7908

**Highwood Motel**
11373-20 Avenue
Tel: 562-8888

## CROWSNEST

**Inn on the Border**
Alberta-B.C. border, Highway 3
Tel: 563-3101

**Kozy Knest Kabins**
West end of Crowsnest Lake on Highway 3
Tel: 563-5155

**McCabe Log Cabin Rentals**
Crowsnest
Tel: 564-4404

## COLEMAN

**Grand Union Hostel**
7719-17 Avenue
Tel: 563-5227

**Stop Inn Motel**
8322-20 Avenue
Tel: 562-7381

**Valley View Motel**
East end, Highway 3
Tel: 563-5600

# *CAMPGROUNDS*

## LUNDBRECK

**Lundbreck Falls** (3 km west of Lundbreck on Highway 3A)
Shelter, fireplaces, firewood, picnic tables, water and toilets. Fishing and swimming are available. There are no trailer hook-ups.

## BURMIS

**Hiawatha Campground** (Highway 507, 1.6 km south of Highway 3, then follow signs) This private campground has 70 sites. Amenities include concession, laundry, showers, flush toilets, shelters, hiking trails. Hook-ups for trailers.

**Castle River Falls** (Highway 507, 18 km south and 5 km west of Burmis)
This campground has 26 units. Fireplaces, firewood, water and toilets. Fishing is available. There are no trailer hook-ups.

## BLAIRMORE

**Crowsnest Campground** (west end of 20 Avenue)
This private campground has 110 sites, 45 with hook-ups. Amenities include heated pool, hot showers, convenience store, playground.

## COLEMAN

**Allison Creek** (1.6 km north of Highway 3 on Highway 940)
This campground has 29 sites with fireplaces, firewood, picnic tables, toilets and water. There are no trailer hook-ups.

**Chinook Lake** (3 km north of Highway 3 on Allison Creek road)
Thirty-four sites, shelters, fireplaces, firewood, picnic tables, toilets and water. There is a beach with a boat launch and fishing available. There are no trailer hook-ups.

## CROWSNEST

**Island Lake** (14 km west of Coleman on Highway 3)
This 5-unit campground has a shelter, fireplaces, firewood, picnic tables, water and toilets. A boat launch and fishing are available. There are no trailer hook-ups.

## FISHING SPOTS

Stocked and natural populations of trout make the waterways of the pass a fisherman's delight.

**Allison Creek**
Rainbows and cutthroats. Enters Crowsnest River near Sentinel on Highway 3.

**Allison Reservoir**
Rainbows and cutthroats are stocked annually. No motorboats allowed. Located 5 km along Allison Creek road north of Highway 3.

**Blairmore Creek**
Rainbows, cutthroats, brookies. Creek joins Crowsnest River at west edge of Blairmore.

**Burmis Lake**
Rainbows. No motorboats allowed. Located near Burmis between Highway 3 and Crowsnest River.

**Coleman Fish & Game Dam**
Rainbows. Located 2 km north of Coleman.

**Crowsnest Lake**
Rainbows and rockies, lake trout, cutthroats. Located 8 km west of Coleman on Highway 3. Boat launch.

**Crowsnest River**
Rainbows, browns, rockies, bull trout. Parallels Highway 3 through the pass. Minimum size limits, seasonal closures. Bull trout limit is 0.

**Emerald Lake**
Cutthroats. Stocked annually. No motorboats. Located 10 km west of Coleman on Highway 3.

**Frank Lake**
Rainbows. There is a widening of the Crowsnest River formed by the Frank Slide located near Frank on Highway 3.

**Island Lake**
Rockies, cutthroats, brookies. Both sides of Highway 3 between Crowsnest and Hazell at west end of the pass.

**Lees Lake**
Rainbows. Located 2 km south on Highway 507. Private. Fee charged to park. Maximum boat speed of 12 km/hr.

**McGillivray Creek**
Rainbows, cutthroats. North side of Highway 3 at Coleman.

**Phillipps Lake**
Rainbows, cutthroats. Access via Rumrunners' Run hike.

**Star Creek**
Rainbows, brookies, bull trout, rockies. Access via Star Creek falls hike.

**Window Mountain Lake**
Rainbows, cutthroats. Terminus of Window Mountain lake hike.

**York Creek**
Rainbows, rockies. Confluence with the Crowsnest River 1 km west of Blairmore.

## GOLF COURSES

**Crowsnest Pass Gold & Country Club**
10701-24 Avenue
Blairmore
Tel: 562-2776

# Index

*Jane Ross and William Tracy on Tent Mountain. Mount Ptolemy behind. Photo Michelle Tracy.*

## ABOUT THE AUTHORS

Author **Jane Ross** is trained as an historian and has worked in the heritage resources field for 25 years. She has written several social studies textbooks and historical monographs. Jane has hiked in Baffin Island, Greenland, New Zealand and the Canadian Rockies. She coauthored *The David Thompson Highway: A Hiking Guide.*

**William Tracy's** MA in anthropology has given him a keen interest in the ethnology of historic areas. A native of Bangor, Maine, he has resided in western Canada for the past 23 years and is currently employed as senior planning advisor for Heritage Resource Management of the department of Community Development. He was the planner for both the Frank Slide Interpretive Centre and Leitch Collieries Provincial Historic Site since their inception.